IN TOO DEEP

Teens Write About Gangs

By Youth Communication

Edited by Al Desetta

IN TOO DEEP

EXECUTIVE EDITORS
Keith Hefner and Laura Longhine

CONTRIBUTING EDITORS
Philip Kay, Andrea Estepa, Marie Glancy, Clarence Haynes,
Carol Kelly, Nora McCarthy, and Hope Vanderberg

LAYOUT & DESIGN
Efrain Reyes, Jr. and Jeff Faerber

COVER ART
James Faber

Copyright © 2009 by Youth Communication®

All rights reserved under International and Pan-American Copyright Conventions. Unless otherwise noted, no part of this book may be reproduced, stored in a retrieval system, or transmitted in any form or by any means, electronic, mechanical, photocopying, recording, or otherwise, without express written permission of the publisher, except for brief quotations or critical reviews.

For reprint information, please contact Youth Communication.

ISBN 978-1-933939-75-9

Second, Expanded Edition

Printed in the United States of America

Youth Communication®
New York, New York
www.youthcomm.org

Table of Contents

Rebels Without a Cause, *Anonymous* 11
    The writer spends two days with his old gang and writes about their partying, random gunplay, and seemingly suicidal lives.

Whatever Become of the Untouchables?, *Anonymous* 18
    In a follow-up to the previous article the writer learns the fate of his former gang members.

My Boyfriend Was a (Latin) King, *Anonymous* 22
    The writer won't stay with her boyfriend if he stays in the Latin Kings.

Down With the Decepts, *Christopher Bogle* 28
    Christopher joins a dangerous gang when he's 13. After going to jail and seeing a relative killed in the drug trade, he turns his life around.

My 'Gang-Related' Weekend, *Anonymous* 41
    After a violent confrontation with rival gang members and other close calls, the writer is happy to return to her group home.

The Real Deal on Gangs, *Anonymous* 46
    The writer interviews three teens who are members of the Bloods, La Familia, and the Latin Kings.

Crewsin' for a Bruisin', *Troy Shawn Welcome* 51
    Troy gives a "who's who" of typical gang characters.

Contents

The Life and Times of a Decepticon, *David Quiles Guzman* 57
  David interviews a former female member who
  describes her descent into the gang lifestyle and how
  she managed to escape.

Remembering Mike, *Carlos Lavezzari* 61
  Carlos reflects on an incident in the schoolyard that
  robbed him of one of his closest friends.

In Too Deep, *Phillip Hodge* 63
  Philip interviews two former gang members about the
  costs of being down.

The Last to Know, *Anonymous* 69
  The writer discovers her boyfriend has joined a gang.

Almost One of the Gang, *Anonymous* 75
  Although many of his friends are gang members, the
  writer decides not to join.

My Crew Was My Family, *Xavier Reyes* 80
  Xavier, 13, runs away from an abusive home and lives
  on the streets. His street friends become his new family.

When Things Get Hectic, *Juan Azize* 92
  Juan is torn between watching his friends' backs and
  staying out of trouble.

True Love Won't Die, *Betty Dominguez* 96
  Betty and Frank join a gang and get caught up in
  violence.

Contents

FICTION SPECIAL: The Fallen, *Paul Langan* 103

Teens: How to Get More Out of This Book 112

How to Use This Book in Staff Training 113

Teachers and Staff: How to Use This Book In Groups 114

Credits 116

About Youth Communication 117

About the Editors 120

More Helpful Books from Youth Communication 122

Introduction

Gangs are a fact of life in too many neighborhoods. As one writer in this book puts it, "Violence surrounds us everywhere: school, work, even in front of your crib. Kids nowadays are ready to kill each other over the dumbest things."

In this book, 13 teens write from first-hand experience about Crips, Bloods, Latin Kings, and other gangs, shedding light on the issues they struggle with. While adults tend to see gangs as universally negative, these stories show how gangs fill a need in some teens—for acceptance and respect, for a group to belong to, for protection in violent neighborhoods.

As Christopher Bogle writes in "Down With the Decepts," his account of joining a notorious gang at age 13:

"I felt love when the members were giving me pounds and accepting me as a member of their crew. I knew they had my back and I had theirs. I wouldn't have traded that feeling for anything."

But gangs, of course, also come with a cost, one that isn't always obvious at first. Christopher eventually ends up in jail, along with many of his crew members. In "Rebels Without a Cause," the anonymous writer returns to a gang he once belonged to, and is struck by the random violence of the members' lives. In a follow-up story written two years later, he provides an account of what became of them—some escaped that life, and some didn't.

These stories also explore the impact of gang violence on bystanders, as well as friends and family of gang members. In "Remembering Mike," the author tells how a friend was killed by gang members over talking to a girl. In "True Love Won't Die," Betty Dominguez loses her boyfriend, a gang member, in a fight with a rival gang.

Weighing the appeal of gang membership against its costs isn't always easy, and several stories show this conflict. Growing up in a neighborhood that has become a battleground for gang violence, Juan Azize is torn between watching his friends' backs and staying out of trouble. Another writer looks on as his friends join the Crips, but he stands by his decision to not go along with them.

In all of these stories, the writers reckon with the real pressures and lures of gangs, while providing an unflinching look at gang violence. Their stories have the authenticity and power that only eyewitnesses can provide.

In some stories, names and identifying details have been changed.

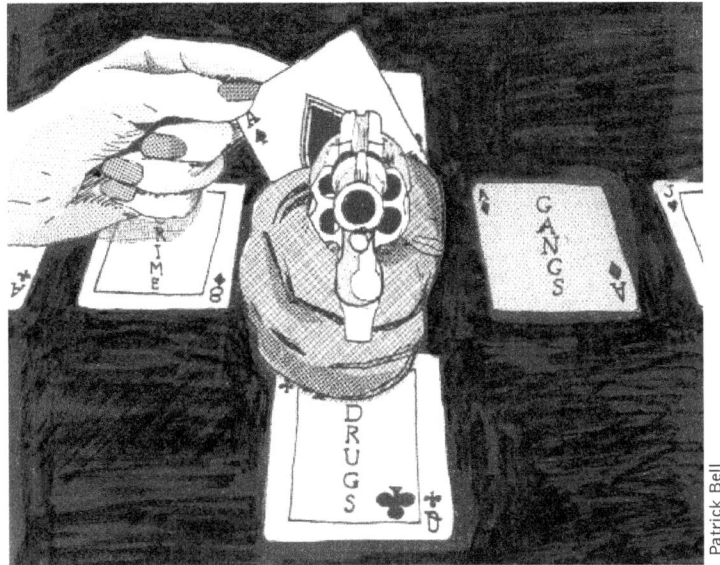

Rebels Without a Cause: Two Days With a Posse

By Anonymous

It was a Monday night when I returned to a posse called the Untouchables. I hadn't hung out with them in almost a year, because I had decided to stay out of trouble. I had been down with this gang for about two years.

My friend Chris accompanied me. His cousin Ace is the leader of the Untouchables. About 10 o'clock that night we went to the project where Ace lives.

Over 10 years ago Ace's parents were killed in a freak car accident. From that time on Ace and his sisters took care of themselves. Now age 20, he still lives in his parents' four-room apartment with his sisters Denise and Doris. Their oldest brother Mike is in the army, but sends money to them.

Chris told Ace that we wanted to stay for a few days. Ace said

In Too Deep

"no problem" and allowed us to sleep on his couches.

Ace's project looked like it had been through a war. The doors to the building's main lobby had been broken off, park benches were worn out, and graffiti were written on most of the apartment buildings.

Their place was a pigsty. The dishes looked like they had been in the sink for decades. Beer bottles were scattered on the floor, roaches were all over the place. There were so many roaches that you could sit down and have a conversation with them.

Ace went out, leaving me and Chris. Chris started talking about how Ace lived.

"He's a total renegade, a rebel. He blames his parents for leaving him at the age of 10, he blames his brother. He blames everybody for the life he now leads. He never even made it to high school."

Ace's sister Denise then came into the crib dressed in a very short skirt. She was surprised to see Chris and me. She hugged him and kept saying, "Long time no see," and, "What ya been up to?"

After a quick discussion, I went outside to call my mother. I told her it was too late to come home and that I was going to stay at a friend's house.

Sleeping at Ace's apartment was impossible. I saw a mouse in the middle of the living room floor eating some sort of meat. I picked up my shoe and threw it at him. Chris was sleeping on the other couch. I couldn't sleep a wink.

Around noon everybody was getting up. I heard someone in the kitchen. I got up, put on my shoes, and went in. It was Ace's older sister, Doris. She was washing dishes.

She was surprised to see me after such a long time. She hugged me and asked if I was hungry. I said, "Hell, yeah." She threw me a box of Fruity Pebbles and said, "Enjoy."

I asked her when she came in and she said, "Just a few minutes ago. Out partying, ya know. Gotta get paid."

She continued to wash the dishes. She asked me questions like: What have I been up to? Where have I been?

I said, "Everything. . . and all over."

She started laughing. "You're stupid, ya know that?"

Then Ace walked through and told me and Chris to come on.

I spent the rest of the afternoon with other members of the Untouchables—Q-Tip, K-Born, and Trent. We all sat around and told stories about girls, people we knew, and things we saw on TV. I realized they had no sense of time—some of them didn't even know the day of the week.

That night, Ace decided to throw a party in a vacant apartment that belonged to a old lady who recently passed away. Ace, Chris, and I went to get the sound equipment. We took the equipment out in the hallway and were waiting for the elevator when Ace's sister Doris told him something and he told Chris to come with him.

I realized they had no sense of time—some of them didn't even know the day of the week.

They were about to run down the stairs when I shouted, "What about the equipment?"

Ace threw me a small Gucci bag and said, "Hold this. And if anybody try to take the equipment, use it. We'll be back in 15 minutes."

Fifteen minutes! Yeah right, he meant an hour.

Anyway, I sat down on one of the speakers and looked into the bag. There was a .38 Special inside, and it was somewhat old.

An hour passed and they returned with pizza. Chris gave me a slice while Ace ran into the house with K-Born. Me and Chris waited in the hallway for a few minutes eating pizza. Then I went inside to wash my hands.

When I went in I saw nothing but crack capsules on the coffee table. Ace and K-Born were dividing them up.

The party started around 8 o'clock that night. Members of two other gangs were there. I met students from four different high schools. I couldn't believe they were partying on a Tuesday night—a school night.

Chris went and got the forties (Old English, of course) and we all got drunk. (Well, I got drunk a little.) I remember I was cracking jokes about how small the apartment was.

Then this guy named Jay tried to start a fight with me. Lucky for him, Chris got in the way or I would have had to do some damage.

Suddenly Mel Qwan came running, telling everyone there was a shooting outside. Everybody ran downstairs like a herd of cattle. It turned out to be a false alarm. Some went back to the party, but most sat downstairs on the benches talking, drinking, and play fighting.

Then, to my surprise, Ace told me to go sell some crack capsules for him and gave me a handful (about 15 capsules.)

"Whatever ya make, ya can keep half," he said.

I was about to tell Ace that I didn't want to do it, but then Chris got up and said, "I'll take him to the big park." Once out of sight I gave the capsules to Chris and he took care of them.

Around midnight we went back to the party. Things were starting to quiet down when Jay and Ace started pulling out their guns and threatening members of another gang to "Get the $^#%$^ out or get us some," from a girl they knew, but then things got squashed because they all were drunk.

Around two o'clock the party was over and Ace, Chris, and I fell asleep in the vacant apartment. We slept against the wall and on the floor.

I got up around 10:30 and went upstairs to Ace's house and ate some breakfast with Denise (more Fruity Pebbles). I asked her if she had finished school.

"School? Nah, after the 10th grade I didn't see any reason to go back," she said. "That's when I met Big Red and we started going together. He promised to take care of me."

I asked her where he was now.

"He's in jail," she said, getting up to take her bowl to the sink. "He got arrested seven months ago on drug charges. I haven't seen him since."

I then asked her what she planned to do now.

"I don't know. I just live day by day. Maybe when Big Red gets out we'll leave New York and start a new life elsewhere."

I stared at her as she spoke. She had a lost look about her. She honestly didn't know what to do. I then asked when Big Red would get out.

"Nine years from now," she said.

She got up to answer the phone. Ace then came in alone. I asked him where Chris was and he said, "He went to take care of some unfinished business."

I followed Ace into his room as he started counting his money. I looked in his closet and saw comic books. It was a stack of X-Men. I asked him if he collected them.

"Yeah, every time I get the chance. The X-Men are renegades, too. Just like me. Society is putting them down because they're mutants. The same as we are, because we're black and they think we'll amount to nothin'. We're rebels without a cause, ya know. We're survivors. We take what we need. Yeah, just like Robin Hood. Steal from the rich and give to the poor, which is us."

He continued to count his money.

Around noon we went outside to walk around. I then told him I was leaving later on to take care of some business. He said, "Cool." We went to the store and got something to drink, and then we went up to Q-Tip's house and watched him act stupid.

"Come on, man, ya not gonna look out. I just need one!" he shouted to Ace. "One, man, just one!" Ace kept saying no.

I looked into Q-Tip's eyes as he continued to beg for a crack capsule. I saw nothing. It was like he had empty space in his eyes, and there was nothing but a little glare. Ace got what he came for and we broke out.

"He's another has-been," Ace said. "There's one thing I've learned in this business. The seller may sell it, but never use it, because if he do, he's all messed up." We then went back to his place and watched *All My Children*.

Chris then came back with a Jamaican-looking guy named The Man. I heard he was a big drug dealer in Brooklyn. The Man came in and sat down on the beat-up couch and talked to Ace. Ace gave him an envelope with nothing but twenties in it.

> *"We're rebels without a cause, ya know. Yeah, just like Robin Hood. Steal from the rich and give to the poor, which is us."*

The Man put it aside and continued to talk to Ace. I looked up at Chris. The Man then took out a .44 Magnum automatic. It looked like it just got off the assembly line. He kept shouting: "Me want me money! Me want me money!"

He then got up and shot Ace's VCR right off the television set. The bullet went right through the record button. He turned to Ace and said, "Get me money." He then grabbed the envelope, put his gun away, and left.

Man, was I nervous. For a moment I thought he was going to turn that gun on us. Ace's sister came running into the living room asking what happened. Ace started shouting.

"He's nothin' but a little man. He's a dead man. He not scaring nobody over here. He wanna shoot it out, we can do this, Brutus. Go for one deep [fight head on]." He then picked up his VCR and took it in his room.

I looked at Chris as he just shook his head.

We then went to the big park and watched Ace try to blow off some steam by playing basketball. We told him we were breaking north. He then slapped us a five and said, "Ya know those X-Men books in my closet? Ya can have them. They'll probably do ya some good."

I thanked him, then Chris and I went back to his place to pick up our things. As I got the X-Men books, Chris started talking.

"He's never going to live right. The way he's going, he'll probably end up six feet under." He shook his head. "I don't know, man. I love my cousin, but I can't help but think he's better off dead."

We walked to the train station. I went to night school and finally went home. My mother was happy to see me home safe—she even cooked my favorite meal and baked a cake. She told me how worried she was, and I assured her that I was OK.

After catching up with what my mother and sister had been doing the last two days, I took a shower and went to bed. I sat up most of the night thinking about what had happened. I thought about the Untouchables' suicidal quest to survive, Ace's drug dealing, and that conversation with Denise.

I thought about the time when I was just like Ace, until I decided to change.

But the thing that got me most of all was that look in Q-Tip's eyes—the total emptiness he had on his face. One look at him, and I knew he'd do anything for crack. Even kill.

The author was 19 when he wrote this story. He later ran an after school program for elementary school children.

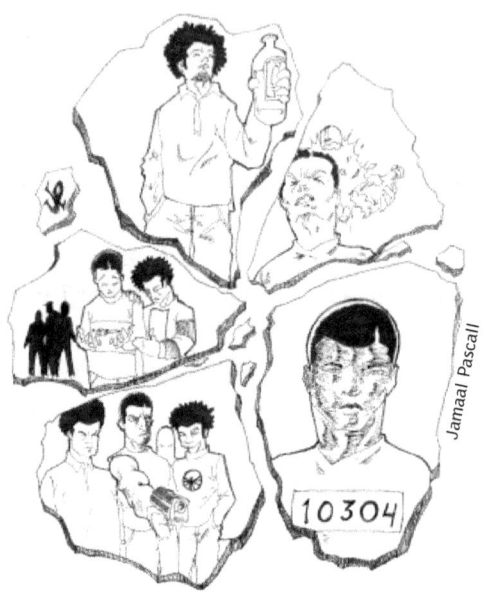

Jamaal Pascall

Whatever Became of the Untouchables?

By Anonymous

Two years ago, I wrote the story you just read about my old posse, called the Untouchables. In just two days with them I saw enough to write a novel.

On a hot Sunday morning last summer, I sat down on a milk crate at my friend Chris's unfurnished apartment. With his help, I pieced together the story of what happened to this gang over the past two years. Chris is a cousin of Ace, their leader.

Roll call: Ace, the leader of the pack. K-born, the enforcer. Q-Tip, the crackhead, and Trent, the lover. They hung out all night and slept all day. They once threw a party in a dead lady's apartment (on a school night at that). They beat up high school kids, shoplifted, sold drugs, and collected comic books. That was an average day for the Untouchables.

When I wrote the story, my main focus was Ace, their leader, a true renegade. Ever since his parents died when he was only 10, Ace was in and out of trouble. At the age of 15 he dropped out of school and became a drug dealer. For five years he worked for a guy called "the Man."

A few months after my story was printed, the Man was arrested for killing three people in Washington, D.C. He's now serving a 25-to-life sentence. With the Man gone, the neighborhood was ripe for the picking. Every dealer in the area wanted to be king. Ace was the likely candidate because of his strong leadership over the Untouchables. But instead of becoming the employer he became an employee and went to work for a new kid—Pierre.

Imagine a 17-year-old, skinny, light-skinned, African-American kid in a white Italian silk suit calling himself Pierre Cardin. He seemed to appear out of nowhere wearing an Armani suit and a smirk on his face—a kid so full of confidence he wasn't afraid of anything the Untouchables could do to him.

With the Untouchables backing him up, Pierre became the neighborhood drug lord. His eight-month reign made a lot of headlines—not his name, just his actions.

Trent was the stone cold Cassanova of the Untouchable's crew. With his good looks he could sweet-talk almost any woman right out of her clothes. Trent had the bad habit of sleeping with other men's girlfriends, and he made a big mistake when he did that to Pierre.

They beat up high school kids, shoplifted, sold drugs, and collected comic books. That was an average day.

Her name was Shanique. Many say Pierre truly loved that girl, but she didn't care squat about him—just his money. When he learned that Shanique had slept with Trent, he hired some Panamanian kid to kill him.

Days later, Trent went to a local barbershop to get a haircut. While sitting in the barber's chair, a masked kid came in and shot him in the face. When the police arrived to question the people who witnessed the shooting, they all said they saw nothing.

With Trent's death, the Untouchables disbanded and Pierre had total control of the neighborhood drug trade. A month later, three Panamanians were gunned down in front of a grocery store. The shooters were believed to have been Haitian. The incident sparked an all-out war.

The Panamanians tried to retaliate. They shot several people hanging out in front of a building. It turned out none of them were Haitian.

A couple of weeks later things quieted down. Many people still believe Pierre started the war because he was afraid the police would find out the truth about Trent's death.

Trent had the bad habit of sleeping with other men's girlfriends, and he made a big mistake when he did that to Pierre.

Ace was the only one of the group who kept his own set pattern. At 1 o'clock he was always in front of the TV watching *All My Children,* and three times a day—every morning, noon and night—he ate a bowl of Fruity Pebbles cereal. Ace had never seemed to me to be a follower. He hated taking orders from the Man and now he worked for Pierre, who was three years younger than him.

Six months ago, Ace and Pierre drove to Georgia in a rented car to pick up a small shipment of cocaine. On the way back to New York, Pierre was driving drunk and a pair of state troopers pulled them over for speeding.

The way Chris tells it, when they asked him for his driver's license, Pierre replied, "I never got one." The state troopers realized he was drunk and told them both to get out of the car. They then searched the car and found a bag of pure cocaine and two MAC-10 handguns.

Pierre and Ace claimed they never saw the stuff before and that they had borrowed the car from a friend. They were taken to the local police station where the troopers learned that the car had been rented with a stolen credit card. They are now serving six years each in a Georgia prison.

All this happened in less than six months. With Ace in jail, his brother Mike returned home from the army to look after their sisters Denise and Doris. Doris, Ace's oldest sister, became addicted to crack. Denise decided to stop waiting for Big Red, her boyfriend, to get out of jail. She got her GED and a job at Macy's.

Meanwhile, Q-tip went to a drug rehab center and K-born finished school and went away to college. Today, Q-tip and K-born are both doing quite well. Q-tip is working in a clothing store, the same one he once shoplifted. K-born is starting his third semester in college. He's majoring in accounting.

Many times we were told that drugs were bad for us and that they had the power to destroy our lives. Some of us took those words to heart and got out while we could. The others could only see all that money to be made.

After he finished filling me in on everything that happened, Chris and I shook hands and said goodbye. Walking down the hallway, I saw Ace's graffiti on the wall. It read: "THE UNTOUCHABLES CAN'T BE TOUCHED."

He was wrong.

The author was 21 when he wrote this story.

My Boyfriend Was a (Latin) King

By Anonymous

The first time I saw Carlos, I liked the way he looked: Not too tall, brown eyes, black hair, and a nice dresser. He also had an enchanting personality. He was very friendly and used to joke around with everybody, even though he was sometimes a little annoying.

I started hanging out with Carlos and my friend Katherine in the 9th grade. We used to go out for lunch almost every day. The three of us became best friends and we looked out for each other. If one of us had a problem, we always tried to help in any way we could.

After two years of friendship, Carlos and I started talking about having a closer relationship. In the fall, he asked me to go out. I said yes!

At first I felt really strange, because one day he was my friend and the next day my boyfriend. But I gave myself some time.

Our relationship at that time was pretty good. We had a couple of fights, but nothing big. I always thought that having a serious relationship was easy, and at first it was.

But I kept hearing Carlos make comments about gangs and it surprised me, because our school is pretty tame. He would constantly shout, "A.D.R." ("amor de rey" or love of the king). Carlos said he didn't have anything to do with gangs, but that his brother had a high position with the Latin Kings.

I wasn't fully convinced, though. Once he told me he had been thinking of becoming a Latin King.

I think he was looking for support, because his father was in jail in his native country and his mother drank a lot. Katherine and I convinced him not to join, or so I thought. He agreed with us that gangs weren't a solution to his problems. He said he was only thinking about joining because of his older brother. They are best friends and Carlos looks up to him.

But then, three months after we began dating, he got into a fight. He didn't tell me anything. I found out from Katherine.

It was a stupid fight. He just saw a person from another gang,

Carlos told me he had been thinking of becoming a Latin King.

he said. I was very suspicious because it was becoming obvious that Carlos was involved in a gang. But every time I asked him, the answer was, "No."

Another time, Katherine made a comment about an argument he had with gang members and I started asking her questions about it. She told me that Carlos was indeed part of the Latin Kings, and that he got into another fight because he was trying to leave the Kings. Carlos didn't want to tell me anything because he knew I didn't like those kinds of "groups."

I never liked gangs. I feel that most kids get into them because they feel lonely, with no support from family and friends. They find a bunch of people who supposedly care about them and their problems. But gangs become dangerous when members get to the point where they're not themselves, and have to follow rules and orders from another person.

Carlos' plan was to leave the gang without me knowing he ever was part of one. From what I heard from my friends, he didn't want to be part of the Kings because he really cared about our relationship. He knew there was no way I could accept him being part of a gang.

But even though he was trying to protect me, I was hurt because he wasn't honest with me. I knew something was going on. But deep inside I wanted to believe him when he said he had nothing to do with gangs.

After I found out what he was up to, I didn't know what to do. I was depressed, worried, and, most of all, disappointed. A couple of weeks passed and I didn't tell him what I had found out. I just didn't know what to do or say.

I couldn't end the relationship because I really cared for him and it's not like he was a bad person. He treated me great and was always a gentleman.

But I also had this anger toward him that didn't let me breathe. His dishonesty really hurt me because it showed that I didn't have the right to know what was happening with him. The secret part of him wasn't his bright side, but it was part of his life.

If he had trouble getting out of the gang, at least I could have been there supporting him. It's always easier to go through a hard time with a friend or a loved one.

As I was trying to figure out how I felt, things got worse. A week after Katherine told me Carlos was in a gang, somebody told my mother that he was part of the Kings.

After my mother found out, she forbade me to see Carlos anymore. She thought that being with a "street boy" could get me in trouble.

After my mother found out, I told Carlos that I knew he was in a gang. He told me that it's very difficult to get out of one because they share information that only members are allowed to know. Once you're in, you're supposed to be a member for life.

I told him that we couldn't see each other for a while. We didn't argue about the situation with my mother. He understood that she was concerned about me.

Even though I was really mad, I understood his situation and how bad he was feeling. I couldn't hate him for not being honest, but I needed time to forgive. I was very upset, and I didn't want to have a relationship with a person who didn't trust me to share his bad times as well as good times.

It was hard to tell him, but I needed time to figure things out. And Carlos needed time to decide what he wanted and to solve his problems. He respected my decision, but he was very angry.

At first, he didn't want to talk to me at all, which again made me feel disappointed that he was acting so immature. Then a week passed and he started saying "Hi." We started being friends again.

> *I knew he made a mistake by getting involved in a gang, but I couldn't just walk away from him.*

I wasn't allowed to talk to Carlos or even see him, but we were in the same school so it was impossible not to. And besides, we still liked each other. I knew he made a mistake by getting involved in a gang, but I couldn't just walk away from him.

Then one day, a month after we split up, he was officially out. The Kings stopped bothering him because his brother was one of the leaders.

Even though I had broken up with Carlos, my feelings changed. I really liked this guy. He was not a bad person, although he had lived a pretty ugly life. But he learned from his mistakes and was trying to organize things in his life.

Carlos and I started dating again after Valentine's Day. It took a couple of hours of talking and listening to each other to finally get back together.

He told me that he still really liked me, which was part of the reason he got out of the gang. I had thought we would be together again, but I wanted to give myself time to think.

I know he won't make the same mistakes as before because I believe in his words. Even if he lied to me before, I believe him now because he has changed so much.

> *I learned to stand up for myself with my boyfriend, and became wiser and stronger emotionally.*

During this last month, Carlos has learned to be a more open person. He doesn't look for trouble and he goes straight to his house after school. Best of all, he isn't hanging out with the wrong crowd. Even his family is doing better. His mother is getting professional help for her drinking problem.

My mother still doesn't want me to see him, so I haven't told her that we got back together.

It's not easy to hide a relationship. Sometimes I'm exhausted and wonder if I made the right decision. It's hard, because if I want to go out I need to make up a story at home. I need to be very careful about what I say when mom asks, "Who gave you that?" If I'm talking to him on the phone, I have to speak as low as possible.

Hopefully, all this sacrifice won't be for nothing. When I look back at the past few months, it's hard not to think of the pain I experienced. But I believe that everything happens for a reason.

I learned to stand up for myself with my boyfriend, and became wiser and stronger emotionally. Maybe what I feel for him now is not love, but maybe it is. Whatever I'm feeling, it's not something that happens every day. That's why I'm sticking like glue to it.

If at some point we have to break up, I just hope it's not for being dishonest. I forgave once, but I'm not going to do it twice. Even if I'm in love with Carlos, it won't matter. There is no reason to make the same mistake twice.

The author was in high school when she wrote this story.

Down with the Decepts

By Christopher Bogle

When I was 13 years old, I joined the Decepticons, one of the most dangerous gangs in Brooklyn. My best friend's brother introduced me to Rob, the leader of the Decepts, when I was on the basketball court around my way. I told him that I wanted to get down with his crew, even though I knew it wasn't going to be easy.

The reason I wanted to get down with them was because they were wearing fly gear and had money in their pockets and were getting mad girls.

To get initiated into the gang, I had to get flipped (jumped) by the other gang members all at one time, to prove my toughness.

I loved to fight, so I was ready to show off my skills. I had lost only two fights since coming to America from Jamaica. Sometimes I would pick fights with kids in my hood because

I could beat them down with no problem. I became a bully in school because I was fed up with the kids picking on me because of the way I talked and dressed.

Rob wanted me to meet him in the park so I could go through my initiation. I told him I would be there to get down for my crown.

The next day, after meeting Rob in the center of the basketball court, mad heads started coming in my direction. I was surrounded by mad brothas and they formed a circle around me. They were swinging on me from every angle. I was knocked to the ground for a moment. I got up with the quickness because I didn't want to be killed. I started swinging, catching mad heads, and they were hitting the floor.

Then I was cracked over the head with a 40-ounce bottle. The bottom of the bottle cracked but I didn't pass out. I took the impact and Rob stopped the fight. He gave me a pound, telling me that I was down with the crew. My tag name was going to be "Iron Head."

Some of the members started giving me pounds and welcoming me to the family of the Decepts. I got respect from the members I fought. It was the first time I ever got jumped. I was lucky to still be alive without any bones broken.

When the brothas were giving me pounds, it felt like a family. I hadn't felt like that around my own family in a long time. I wasn't getting the love that most mothers give to their only son. I felt love when the members were giving me pounds and accepting me as a member of their crew. I knew they had my back and I had theirs. I wouldn't have traded that feeling for anything.

I met Rob around his block, so I could get introduced to the rest of the gang. There were mad brothas there talking among themselves. I was introduced as the newest member.

After the meeting, Rob told me to come upstairs to his crib because he had to give me something very important.

I was sitting on the couch when Rob came out of his room with a .25 handgun. He told me it was now mine to keep for protection from other rival gangs. I hesitated to take the gun from him until he told me almost every member got one.

Then Rob told me I was a member of the Decepts for life and there was no way that I could leave. He also said if I ever betrayed him, he would kill me in a heartbeat. He said I was going to be his main man because he liked what he saw in the park that day.

I had never held a gun in my life, but I saw my cousin's gun and guns on television. I knew having one gave you power. I started carrying the .25 for protection because so many brothas were getting killed in my hood.

> *I knew they had my back and I had theirs. I wouldn't have traded that feeling for anything*

When I became a member of the Decepts, it gave me a second family. I was having mad problems with my mother that I tried my best to avoid by staying out of the house. My sisters were wearing fly gear that my mother bought for them, but she wasn't buying gear for me because of the problems we were having. I had to go out there to get paid to get the fly clothes and the $100 sneakers that everybody in the hood was wearing.

The next couple of days I was chilling on the block with the crew when I started to become bored. My pockets were broke and I needed loot to buy some sneakers. Rob told me that we were going out to rob people.

That same night me and Rob and six other heads went to the park to catch a herb. Every head was packing their toast (gun) that night. We couldn't find anybody to rob, so we decided to leave.

When we were walking back to the train station, we spotted a man who was dressed like a businessman. Baby Killer and I went up to him, put the toast in his back, while the other heads looked out for police. He got mad pet (scared) and gave us his wallet with the quickness.

When we got back to the block we saw that the wallet had $280 in it. Baby Killer and I got $80 each and the rest was split up amongst the brothas who took part in the robbery.

When I got $80 in my pocket, it was more than what my mother had spent on me since I turned 13. I started to become greedy for more. I knew when I robbed the man it was wrong, but I really didn't care. I didn't care about nothing but money.

When I got back to the house my mother asked if I went to school. She knew I wasn't going to school because she received letters and phone calls from my teachers. My mother knew I was hanging with gang members because they sometimes rang my bell to come get me.

I told her that I didn't care about school or if I got shot or went to jail for committing a crime. She told me that I would regret those words someday when I was behind bars doing time.

I felt good putting the toast to the other guy's backs. I was starting to like this way of living. I thought I could do this for the rest of my life. I was "the man" because I could pull the trigger. I wasn't scared to pull it if I had to.

After a couple of days of chilling and letting things die down, news came back to the block that Rob's brother had been shot by a rival gang and was in the hospital on life support. I went to the hospital with Rob and the other brothas to see if he was going to make it through. When we arrived, the doctor told Rob that his brother died about an hour before we got there.

Rob angrily walked out the hospital and headed back to his crib. He told us that he was going to settle the score by shooting up the rival gang. He told us to get our guns and meet up on the block at 10 p.m.

It was 10:30 when we started driving to the other gang's neighborhood. The streets were dirty with a lot of garbage on the sidewalk. There were burned-out buildings and some had graffiti written on them. There weren't a lot of people outside, but there were mad heads from the rival gang hanging on the corner. Rob told me to look out for the police while he handled his business. Lethal and Face kept the car warm for our getaway. Rob wanted us to come from different angles shooting, because he didn't want to leave anybody alive while his brother was six feet deep.

When I saw Rob pull out his toast, I knew it wasn't going to be a good night.

When the shooting started, mad heads were running for cover to protect themselves from getting hit. The rival gang members were shooting back. I knew we were winning the war because all the heads from the other gang were getting buck (shot) from left to right. But when I saw Baby Killer get hit, I knew it was time to be out.

I jumped in one of the rides. Lethal and Face drove the car while other heads jumped in. Then Rob jumped in the ride, bragging about seeing the other gang heads drop like a bad habit.

> **My mother came to court that day. She was sad to see her only son chained up like an animal.**

We drove back to our neighborhood. Rob told two heads to drive the car someplace and dispose of it.

Baby Killer died, along with three other people. The shooting was on the TV news that night.

I went to my crib and locked the doors to my room. I was scared seeing so many heads get killed. I was locked in my room for mad days. Sometimes my mother would knock on my door to see if I was alright.

After a couple of days in the crib, I grabbed my toast and my jacket and headed towards the block.

I went to Rob's crib to chill and make sure that he was alright. He told me that he was going to start pushing crack in the area.

But first he wanted to cool out in his crib with his family and let things lie down. He wanted me to be his main man, doing some deliveries, doing hand-to-hand, and watching out for police. I told him that I was down with the idea because it was my chance to make a lot of money.

After a couple of weeks of pushing the drugs, money was coming in like crazy. I was making at least a G ($1,000) a night. The Jamaicans on Franklin Ave. wanted to do business with Rob. I made the deliveries to them and picked up the money.

At the end of the week Rob always hit me off with $400. I spent my money on the latest fly gear, like Tommy Hilfiger, Polo, Gap, and the new kicks.

My mother always asked me where the hell I was getting the money to buy new clothes and sneakers. I told her that my cousin Mickey was buying them for me. She believed me because I had a close relationship with him. Mickey was one of the biggest drug dealers in all of Brooklyn. He had like six crack houses, so my mother knew that he was making loot.

One warm day on the corner I was chilling, doing hand-to-hand with the clientele, and making money. I got bagged by police because they saw me make a sale.

I was taken to the precinct and I called my cousin to come get me. The police let me off because I was young and they couldn't really keep me for just making a sale. I was released to my cousin because I told them that he was my legal guardian. Mickey promised me that he wasn't going to tell my mother, but if I got in trouble again, he was going to %&^&$* me up.

Rob put somebody else on selling the crack while I took a break. I was supposed to stay away from the crack until the police stopped patrolling the area. I was glad because I knew the police would be watching me.

But I wasn't going to let the police stop me from getting paid, so I started robbing people at night and did deliveries any time

Rob wanted me to.

My man and I planned to do a robbery one night. We didn't want anyone else with us because we would have to split the money too many ways.

We went to an area where the people carried a lot of money. We were both packing toast.

We followed the first victim we laid eyes on. We followed her to her building. She was a young attractive lady who looked like she was coming home from work. I robbed her with my toast while my man looked out for police. The lady screamed and we started to run. A cop car spotted us and police started chasing us.

My boy and I split up so we could dodge the police. I stopped running because I was getting tired. I hid in the bushes of someone's backyard. I knew if I got caught I wasn't going be let off so easily like the first time.

After a couple of hours of hiding, I came out of the bushes and started walking to the train station. While I was walking, a cop car rolled up behind me and told me to stand up against the wall. The lady we robbed was in the back seat of the car. I was arrested for armed robbery.

I was taken to the precinct and put in a holding cell. My mother was called this time instead of my cousin, because I knew this was something my cousin wasn't going to be able to get me out of. I thought I was going to Rikers Island with the big boys. I was scared to death because I heard a lot of rumors about the Island. One of them was that they rape other inmates and take their most valuable things.

I was taken to the Spofford Juvenile Detention Center in the Bronx until it was time go to court to face the judge. I saw a lot of Decepticons in that joint. The majority of the kids in Spofford were involved in gangs.

I was handcuffed and shackled when the police brought me in the doors. I was forced to strip naked because I had to get searched for any weapons. They took away my clothes, sneakers, chains, watch—even the gold from my teeth had to be removed. I was given a blue sweater and a pair of blue pants with an old pair of sneakers to wear. The clothes looked bad and the sneakers were skippys from back in the days. I didn't want to wear them but I had to.

They put me in the E-2 dorm with my Decepts from the hood. We had things locked down there. Some of my boys were leaving to go upstate. I didn't want to go anywhere but back on the streets to get paid.

One of the guards woke me up so I could go to court. I was chained up like a dog and transported in the big van that they use to transport killers and robbers to Rikers Island. I was embarrassed to be riding like that. I wanted to have my freedom and not be locked up.

My mother came to court that day and it hurt to have her see me that way. I could tell that she was sad to see her only son chained up like an animal in court. I told her I was sorry for my chaotic behavior.

When my case was called I was nervous standing in front of the judge. My lawyer told me if I took my case to trial and lost, I was going to get more time on my sentencing. If I pled guilty, I was going to get a lesser sentence with a chance to get out on good behavior. I pled not guilty and told my lawyer that I wanted to take my case to trial.

I figured that lady wasn't going to show up because she hadn't been in court. I knew she was still scared about what happened to her. I wanted to take my chances with the trial. If I beat it, I was going to be a free person back in society.

I wanted to go home, but I was sent back to Spofford until my trial date came up. I was ordered by the judge to come back to court in three weeks to start my trial. I was given a chance to speak to my mother for a few seconds before the guard took me back to Spofford. I told my mother that I was sorry for getting myself in trouble with the law.

I lost my case because the lady I robbed came to testify against me. I was upset with myself for thinking she wasn't going to be there. The judge gave me a two-year sentence to do upstate, with the chance to get out early on good behavior.

My mother started breaking down in court. I knew I wasn't going to see my mother for a long time. I was taken back to the holding area to get transported back to Spofford.

I was so upset about what happened in court that I got into a fight with one of the kids in my dorm. They had to move me to another one.

My mother came to see me the week before I was supposed to go upstate. She told me that she wasn't going to be able to visit me if the place was a long way from the city. I told her that I understood and that I wasn't going to be looking for her.

I was taken north to a facility in upstate New York. The program was a structured place because everything was on schedule. I wasn't used to having someone tell me what to do every minute. I knew that I was going to have a lot of problems being locked up.

The place was a secure lock-up for juvenile offenders. When we arrived there, the man told me the staff wouldn't hesitate to rough me up if I got out of hand. I told the man I would defend myself.

My first three weeks there I got into five fights with my peers. They would say something I didn't like and I would punch them in the face. It was a way to take out my frustrations. I was always locked up in the isolation room.

I started getting myself in trouble with the staff because of my mouth and by being disobedient. I was doing whatever I wanted. I refused to go to school on the campus because I never did like school.

One night a staff member named Brown took me into the back room to talk to me about my attitude. He asked me why was

I trying to act like a tough guy. I told him to get out of my face because I didn't want to hear none of his crap.

He punched me in the face. He slammed me on the floor and busted my chin. Then he restrained me and claimed I tried to attack him. He told me that for the rest of my time there he was going to give me a hard time unless I shaped up.

After that incident with Mr. Brown, I started to follow some of the rules and stay away from getting into fights. I tried my best to stay away from him. I wanted to do my time and get back into society so I could get paid.

I was enrolled in the school on the campus. I had to take reading and mathematics tests. I scored very low on both tests. I scored low because I never went to school in the real world. I was embarrassed to hear the lady tell me my scores. I knew I should have done better because I knew I wasn't stupid. I was determined to improve in mathematics and reading.

I had called my mother and she told me that my cousin Winston had been shot dead in Brooklyn over drugs. My other cousin Mickey got locked up for dealing.

After getting off the phone I started going crazy. I had to be restrained by two staff members. I didn't know how to deal with the news my mother told me. Several staff members talked to me and gave me some advice.

My mother arranged with the facility's director for me to be transported to my cousin's funeral in New York City. She wanted me to see how it looked for someone to lay in a coffin. I was taken to my cousin's funeral by my unit worker in handcuffs and shackles. When we arrived, my worker took them off to show respect for my family. He wasn't supposed to take them off, but he did so out of kindness.

It was hard to see my cousin Winston laying dead in his coffin. I couldn't believe it was one of my family members laying there. I never thought violence could take away anybody from my family. I knew if I didn't get my act together, I was going to be the next one laying in the coffin.

In Too Deep

When I got back to the joint up north, I tried to get over the death of my cousin. I started reading books, so I could stay to myself and keep out of trouble. I read books about Malcolm X, Martin Luther King, Jr., Sojourner Truth, Carter G. Woodson, George Washington Carver. I became addicted to reading books about famous black people. Sometimes my teacher would bring me books from her house. I started to improve in mathematics and reading. I won an award for having the highest average at the end of the marking period. It was the first award I ever won in school.

I was starting to feel proud about myself because I was doing well in school. It made me realize that I had the potential to be a good student.

For the first time in my life, I set goals for myself to accomplish when I got back in the world.

My unit director organized a trip to visit a state prison. It was like a "Scared Straight" program. We visited the prison to talk with the inmates so we wouldn't want to go to prison any time in the near future.

It was a scary moment walking into that prison. We were taken to a little room to hear some of the inmates speak about the crimes they committed and about life in prison.

There was this one inmate who reminded me of myself, because when he was my age he did the same things I had done. He grew up on the streets, joined a gang, did drugs, and spent time upstate. He told us that he regretted pulling the trigger while he doing a robbery. The only difference between him and me was that both of my parents were alive. He lost his mother and father to drugs at an early age. He never had anybody to give him advice about life. Compared to him I was the lucky one, because I had the support of my mother and family.

Most of the inmates were locked up for murder and doing

25-to-life. They encouraged us to stay in school and stay away from drugs.

I sat down and thought about all the things I did to the people in society by robbing and beating them up. Those people I was robbing were innocent people who never did anything to hurt me. I wouldn't want anybody to rob or beat up my two sisters. I realized that doing those acts was wrong. I decided I wanted to continue my education by going to college and getting my degree in law.

For the first time in my life, I set goals for myself to accomplish when I got back in the world. I wanted to keep myself out of trouble and get my high school diploma and go to college. I knew that some of the old heads from the crew wanted me to get back down with them. I was going to stay away from them even if they tried to kill me.

My attitude about life was changing. I was starting to realize that money wasn't everything that life offered. I didn't want to have my freedom taken away from me any more. I wanted to have a good life instead of doing things to get me in trouble.

I started to take my education seriously by learning new math and improving my vocabulary. I got recommendations from my teachers to go to a more advanced class while I was there.

My attitude in the dorm changed because I didn't want all the staff to be against me. I wanted to get out that place quick. I knew if I made problems for myself, things would get worse. I made up my mind to do the right thing. I became a better person because my perspective on life changed.

I got out in a year and a half, instead of two years, because I improved myself. When I arrived in New York, my mother was at the train station waiting for me. I was glad to be going home early. I gave her a big hug and kiss on the cheek. I could tell she was glad to see me because she didn't want to let me go. She told me that things were going to get better. I was glad to be going home and getting my freedom back. I didn't have any plans on losing it again so easy.

It took time for me to get used to my family. I had to follow my mother's rules and go to school. I was on probation for six months. If I violated my probation, I was going to be sent back upstate to finish the rest of my time. I had no problem with following my mother's rules.

A couple of years later I graduated from high school, and I've been accepted to the John Jay College of Criminal Justice. I'm determined to achieve my goal of becoming a District Attorney, prosecuting criminals in the State of New York.

Christopher was 18 when he wrote this story. He graduated from college with a degree in Political Science and Sociology.

My 'Gang-Related' Weekend

By Anonymous

It all started on a Sunday night in my neighborhood. There had been trouble involving my two friends Mark and Scott. They are members of the Bloods organization. So when they get into trouble, it isn't any petty "You was talking about my mama" thing. It can get real serious. Sometimes even deadly.

Earlier in the evening, Scott got punched in the face. When he had to defend himself, he was chased into a park known to some as Richmond Park, but that is known to people around my way as "Burger World."

Now, from my experience of hanging out with Bloods, I knew that "Burger" meant "Latin King." And I may not be the smartest person in the world, but I know that if a Blood is caught running alone through the Latin King's territory, he can end up in a sad front-page story in the newspaper.

So Mark, being the thinker of the group and Scott's fellow Blood, decided that we should go and look for him.

But first he thought we should go to Scott's grandmother's house to make sure he wasn't there. We (meaning me, Mark, and a boy named Ernie) headed off to the projects. When we got to the building, a little "welcoming committee" met us—at least 12 boys sitting on a bench. Mark said not to worry about them, but for some reason I knew better.

We went to the third floor and knocked on the door, only to hear that there was no Scott in that house. At that point I was heated. What else could go wrong? Why did I have to ask that question?

As we walked out of the building, it seemed as if every boy who was sitting on that bench got up and started following us. That was the night that Ernie lived up to his name ("Speedy") because every time he saw what looked like beef (meaning problems) he took flight. He was out of there on that mini-bike of his.

> **He told us that he was a Neta, another gang around my way. And that he wanted all Bloods dead.**

But Mark hadn't looked around yet to see what was happening. He feels he shouldn't have to watch his back for anybody. So I let him know that we were being followed. Mark turned to look, then told me to "fix my face."

Mark meant that I shouldn't let anyone know I was afraid. So I took his advice and didn't let it bother me that we were being followed. But when I turned around to look again, I was shocked to see that the boys had stopped following us and were sitting on another bench.

Mark, Ernie (who had returned from his little vacation), and I were on the way back to my building. The boys said it was getting too late and time for me to get back home. On the way back we joked about Ernie running away every time there was beef. He didn't get mad. All he kept saying was, "I came back, didn't

I?" The conversation released the tension we were feeling.

So we didn't even notice that we were already at my building. That's when those damn butterflies came back. Why would I feel that way? What else could possibly go wrong?

I was expecting about 45 boys to come around the corner any minute now. But the only person who came around the corner was a man who looked like he had a little bit too much to drink. As we walked past, the man asked Mark if he knew anything about a boy who got jumped the day before by some Bloods. Mark heard about the boy getting jumped, but he didn't have anything to do with it, so he said no. But I guess the man had his mind already set on who did it. And it didn't help any that Mark was wearing a red shirt.

The guy started breaking on Mark, yelling and screaming about how he just got released after a four-year jail sentence.

Then he asked Mark if he was a Blood. Mark said yes. The guy really flipped his wig. He told us that he was a Neta, another gang around my way. And that he wanted all Bloods dead.

To make matters worse, this big body builder guy rode by on a bike and asked what was wrong. I felt a little safer because maybe he would help us. But when I saw the black and yellow beads he was wearing, I knew he wasn't going to help us. He was a Latin King. And everybody knows that Netas and Latin Kings stick together. Both gangs are about standing up for their Puerto Rican nation. The drunken Neta told the Latin King the whole story, and each word was getting the Neta madder. Then the Neta punched Mark in the face.

Mark threw himself off the bike. When he saw blood leaking down his face, he went crazy. He went straight at the Neta until the Latin King pulled out a gun from under his shirt. Ernie (a.k.a. Speedy) got on his bike and rode for his life. The Latin King started chasing Ernie. Then Mark realized that he had not been punched in the face, but stabbed.

In Too Deep

I had to pull Mark away from the Neta. But when the Neta started chasing us with a knife, I didn't have to do the pulling anymore—I was the one being pulled. When we slammed the door to my building it locked behind us, thankfully in the Neta's face.

That drove him mad. He picked up a brick and tried to smash the door. Mark sat on the stairs and took off his shirt to stop the bleeding. He told me not to worry, that the Neta wasn't going to be able to get into the building. But the next thing I knew, I heard the Neta yelling and his footsteps on the stairs, getting closer to us.

> **Mark realized that he had not been punched in the face, but stabbed.**

Me and Mark ran up the stairs to my apartment. When we got to my door, I must have banged like 50 times really hard. Nobody answered. It was three o'clock in the morning and I realized that nobody was going to answer the door.

We heard the Neta's footsteps pounding on the stairs and I felt like crying. When my mother finally opened the door, Mark and I ran into my apartment.

Then my mother saw Mark's face. She looked like she was about to do cartwheels and back flips. She cleaned his face and tried to stop the bleeding. Then she asked us what happened.

At the end of the long story, she called the police and the ambulance. She said that Mark needed stitches. She also said that if the cut had been a little more to the right, he would have been blinded for life.

When the bleeding stopped and the excitement died down, guess what happened? Speedy (my mistake, Ernie) came in the door without his shirt and mad sweaty. My mother asked him what happened. He said four cars pulled him over and told him to drop his bike. The Latin Kings in the car accused Ernie of stealing the bike and threatened to kill him. He gave them the bike and begged them to leave him alone. My mother told Ernie to calm down and wait for the police.

Not too long later the police arrived and we explained the whole story again. The ambulance came and took Mark to the hospital. We gave a description of the two guys and everything seemed to be getting better. So why did I keep on getting those butterflies in my stomach?

I didn't even want to think of the answer.

I tried to go to sleep but I kept hearing cars riding around my block. I looked out the window and I saw two cars driving the wrong way up a one-way street.

At first I didn't want to get too suspicious. But then I saw the driver wearing the black and yellow beads. I kept looking out my window until the car stopped and they looked right at me.

Oh no, they knew where I lived!

That night I didn't sleep. I had too much on my mind. I was AWOL from my group home, Mark got stabbed, the Latin Kings knew where I lived, and we never found Scott. So when I woke up, the first thing that I wanted to do was to get the hell back to my group home.

But when I looked out my window, the same cars were still riding around my block. I couldn't believe it. I told my mother and she called her job and said she couldn't come in. I stayed home and kept looking out the window.

The cars disappeared. I waited for them to come back, but they didn't. My mother told me to get myself on the train before I had to stay another night.

I took my stuff and ran to that train. I never felt so happy about going back to my group home in my whole life. And for the first time in two days, the butterflies in my stomach went away.

The author was 15 when she wrote this story.

The Real Deal on Gangs

By Anonymous

Bloods, Latin Kings, Crips. With all the bad things we've heard about gangs, I can't imagine anyone wanting to join one.

But although gangs are feared, there is little that is known about them. More and more young people may be joining gangs, but nobody really knows why they are joining. It was very difficult for me to find gang members who were willing to talk. But when I finally found them, they had a lot to say. And some of what they had to say might change your views on gangs.

Joseph, 18, who lives in a group home, said he joined the Latin Kings because he and his family "were having a lot of fights. I really wasn't getting any love from them."

Gerard, 16, said he joined the Bloods for the same reason: "My moms was flipping. She was telling me to do things that I didn't want to do. So I just started hustling with my dogs."

Taz, 16, is not yet a gang member but wants to join. "The Bloods are all about being a family," she said, "sticking together, going out for theirs, and getting that dough. And that is what I'm all about."

But not all teenagers join gangs because of family problems. Napz, 17, who is down with the gang known as La Familia, told me, "My family life was good." Perhaps Napz joined a gang for the same reason that Joseph did: "The Latin Kings are always there for me when I have beef."

Or as Taz told me: "You will always have someone to look out for you, and to be there for you when you need them."

It seems like teenagers join gangs because they want to belong to something and feel like they're special. Sometimes the love that teenagers get from gangs is greater than the love that they receive from their own families.

"We're like a family," Gerard said. "We do everything together, we get money together. I'm going to bang for my dogs and they are going to bang for me."

Or, as Joseph said about the Latin Kings: "They're not *like* my family, they *are* my family."

Taz said she wants to join the Bloods to "get the satisfaction of having another family."

> *"We're like a family. We do everything together. I'm going to bang for my dogs and they are going to bang for me."*

Joseph, Gerard, and Taz are all in the foster care system. For a lot of kids like them, gangs seem like the only way to have a real family. Joseph told me he gained acceptance, love, and respect by joining the Latin Kings. These are things that most teenagers should be getting at home.

When I used to watch movies about gangs, I never saw female members. Today it's different. Every gang I know has girls in it. And sometimes the females are rolling harder the males. So I wondered: is it harder for females to be in gangs?

In Too Deep

Gerard told me that girls in the Bloods get treated the same as the boys. Joseph said the same thing about females in the Latin Kings—they don't get "sexed in" like they do in some other gangs. But Napz said it was harder for girls in La Familia, because the boys expect to have sex with them.

I spoke with a 15-year-old female who goes by the name of "Bloody Jucks." She, of course, is in the Bloods. She said female gang members can't make as much money because they aren't allowed to sell drugs. She said that "Ruby Reds" (or female Bloods) can get cut quicker because male gang members take females as a joke. Bloody Jucks said she has to go through a lot to get respect.

All the gang members told me that once you're in, you're in for life. There's no easy "in and out." And if you try to get out, there can be some very serious results, sometimes even deadly ones.

Joseph told me there is no way out of Latin Kings unless you die. For the La Familia, Napz said you have to ask the leader. If your reason for wanting to get out is a good one, you won't be bothered. But he also added that you might get beat up or killed.

Once you're in, you're in for life. There's no easy "in and out."

Gerard said you get an "X" cut on your face if you leave the Bloods. And when ex-gang members see you, they get to slice you and beat you up.

But hold on—it gets better. Bloody Jucks said you can get blooded out, as Gerard explained with the X. Or you can get out the same way that you got in—if you sliced somebody to get in, you have to get sliced to get out.

Teens join gangs and don't even realize what they're getting themselves into. Then they have the nerve to want to get out. I asked Taz, who hasn't joined yet, if she was worried about getting out: "If I join a gang, it ain't going to be no in-and-out. It's for life."

What good is being in a gang if you don't have an enemy? The Bloods are in conflict with Latin Kings and Crips. The Latin Kings are in conflict with Bloods and some La Familias. And the La Familias are in conflict with Latin Kings. Why is there so much conflict?

"We try to chill, but every time the Crips and Latin Kings see that red scarf they go crazy," Gerard said.

"Once Latin Kings and Familias were together," Napz said. "Then, because of some beef, we split up. Ever since then, we don't click like that."

"Not everyone is at war with each other," Joseph said.

The sad part is that teens in gangs think there's nothing wrong with going to war. They all said they don't regret joining their organizations.

They told me they've robbed stores, gotten involved in shootouts, and cut fellow teenagers. These are things I would regret. But for gang members these are everyday things, and that is sad.

I asked the gang members: "What advice would you give to someone who was thinking about joining a gang?"

"You should grow up and get a job first," said Gerard. "You should not try to repeat what the past did." He meant you shouldn't join a gang because family members or friends joined one.

"Don't do it," Napz said. "Once you join, your whole life is going to change."

"Think about what you are doing first," Joseph said. "Learn more about the nation."

Even though Taz is not a Blood yet, she gave some very good advice.

"Yo, getting into a gang is something that you have to think hard about. You can't do nothing that you are going to regret. If you think that you ain't going to regret it, then do your thing. If not, don't start nothing that you can't finish, 'cause it can get finished for you."

Before you think of doing something stupid, follow the advice of the gang members. Because trying to be with the "in crowd" can get you with the "dead crowd."

The author was 15 when she wrote this story.

Crewsin' For a Bruisin'

By Troy Shawn Welcome

Are you in a crew? If you are, you know that a lot of crews live a fast life and their actions sometimes lead to a fast death.

For starters, the more people you're with, the more attention you're going to attract. And then most teenagers aren't conscious of what they're doing half the time and don't take the time to reflect. Reflecting on what I've done is one way that I notice my mistakes and correct them before they can negatively affect my life.

Thinking about my own experiences in a crew led me to make up this example of how a typical crew might get themselves into trouble.

It's Friday night and the crew is chillin' on the corner. Jay, who's known for stealing cars, doing stick-ups, and robbing bodegas when he's hungry, is sitting on a car rolling a blunt.

Rob, nick-named Nitty for the character from the movie *The Untouchables* because he's the man you call when you need somebody killed, is passing around a forty to be tapped.

Jeff, who's the one that everybody goes to when they want to discuss an idea for a jack, is coming down the block. They call him the Intelligent Hoodlum, the brain of the crew.

Danny, Jack, and Paul, who are always there for the blunt but for the beef they always front, are scattered on the corner. Jay, Rob, and Jeff hardly ever hang out with the other three guys. You only see Danny, Jack, and Paul when the rest of the crew needs them for something.

> **Danny, Jack, and Paul are always there for the blunt, but for the beef they always front.**

"Yo, Jay!" says Rob.

"What yo?" answers Jay.

"I'm trying to roll this!"

"Yo, here comes Jeff," says Rob.

As Jeff approaches the corner, a group of guys who are new to the area are walking towards him. Jeff walks through the crowd and gets shoved around like a bumper car. He turns around and confronts the last guy to bump him.

"What's the problem?" he asks.

"N-gga, you got something to say!" someone says from the middle of the crowd. "If you want it, it's here."

These guys have no idea that Jeff's boys are right on the corner. And Jeff's crew hasn't seen what's happening down the block.

"Yo Rob, I thought you said that Jeff was coming," says Jay, as he seals the blunt with his lips and tongue. "Where he at?"

Rob looks down the block.

"Yo, some fools is tryin' to mess with my man," he says as he grabs his nickel-plated nine from his car and runs towards Jeff.

"Right where, n-ga? Oh damn!"

Jay throws the blunt into the car, grabs his gun. "Yo D', yo Paul, yo J, it's on, it's on!" He runs over to Jeff.

Danny, Jack, and Paul can see what's going on but they don't immediately follow Jay and Rob.

"Yo, it's mad n-ggas over there," says Danny. "Yo, c'mon J', you going or what?"

"Yo, I think this n-gga Jack is a herb!" says Paul laughing. "Yo, c'mon ya'll, I don't know about you but I ain't going out like a herb."

That's what he says, but what he's actually thinking is: "These n-gas could beat my butt. I don't think I could handle these guys. But if I don't go then everybody will think that I'm a herb. But I'm not. I'll go, but if anything happens I'm out."

It's usually the guys that boast the most who are hiding something, because they're not secure with themselves. So while they're saying "Don't mess with me 'cause I'll bus' ya one!" they're thinking, "If this kid hits me, I don't know what I'm going to do."

Jay, Rob, and Jeff are about to get into a fight with the opposing crew. Jack, Paul, and Danny are waiting in the background.

Now stop and think for a minute about what just happened. Both crews feel they are being disrespected. Jeff was bumped around and no one said as much as a "pardon me." The person who did the bumping feels like he's being challenged. And he must prove to his boys and to Jeff that he's no herb—that no one is allowed to test him. Meanwhile, Jeff's crew sees one of its own outnumbered. How could this whole thing have been avoided?

One way is if Jeff realized that walking through the middle of the opposing crew could cause problems. Some people will think this is the herb's way out—but would you rather take the herb's way out or the body-bag out?

He also could have talked his way through it. I'm not suggesting that he should say, "Chill yo, you the man, I don't wanna mess with you," or "Alright, you got it and I don't want it." There are other ways to talk through a situation.

He could just say, "Excuse you, my man," and keep walking.

Someone might say something to him, but he doesn't have to get into a confrontation. He could just keep walking and pretend that nothing happened.

I know some of you are still saying that you don't want to go out like a sucka. But if you're secure with yourself, you won't need to prove that you deserve respect from a stranger in the street.

And then there's the problem of the guns. If these people didn't have guns they would handle it differently. Guns are a fool's way of dealing with problems. They give people the nerve to go out and kill—and to get themselves and their friends killed. Remember that it's better to live to talk about what happened, than to die and be remembered as the guy who got slaughtered for a ridiculous cause—a bump in the night.

> **How many more of us must die, be caged, or be hospitalized for saying, "What you looking at?"**

I want my peers—especially my African-American brothers—to start thinking more about their actions and the consequences of those actions. Why was your boy shot the other day? Did he lose his life for a stare, a bump, or a battle of the egos? How many more of us must die, be caged, or be hospitalized for saying, "What you looking at?"

Guns, buddah, and forties are all becoming a way of life—they're also a prelude to death!

The True Gangsta

He walks down the streets, strutting his stuff as if he controls everything and everyone in sight, the one who's always saying, "Whatever, I don't give a $^#%$!" He gives the crew all its ideas. He might say, "Yo, let's do this n-gga" or "I feel like jacking somebody, yo."

The rest of the crew almost always goes along with whatever this character wants to do, because if they challenge his corrupt ideas they might be called a herb. He lives life for money, women, guns, and more money. If someone tries to dis him, he must get respect from them before he walks on. But things don't always run smoothly for this character.

There might be two true gangstas in a crew and if there are, they get into conflict a lot. One will say, "Let's do this," and the other might say, "Let's do that." They both feel that they are the biggest and baddest, and so they must fight for their position. It's sometimes more interesting when there are two of these individuals, but one is a handful. Although these characters are very street smart, they're not really intellectuals. But if you find one who is, he could be very dangerous because he has the intelligence to understand his own power and control a crew.

The Intelligent Hoodlum

Many crew members can smell a D-T (undercover-cop) from a mile away or make some money playing cilo (dice). But only a few possess the ability to think clearly and talk their way out of a tight situation.

Every crew has at least one of these. He uses his intelligence to better the schemes of the crew. Any time that the crew decides to do something, everybody instinctively waits for him to give his opinion. He's usually the one who thoroughly examines most of their schemes. He looks at both sides of a situation, sees what can go wrong and how to better the plan.

If the crew has beef, he's the one who thinks more about how to get out of the situation, so they can come back to get revenge, rather than how to prove who's the bigger man. After he has improved their present scheme, he almost always goes along with the plan.

Joe Borderline

He lives the crew life but isn't sure whether he wants to die from it. He loves guns but sees the consequences that guns bring. He loves alcohol but sees that every time they drink, the crew always gets into trouble. He wants to have a better life, but doesn't really want to leave the fellas. He likes the advantages of the fast life, but knows that it can lead to danger. He doesn't know if he should change his life or continue to roll with the crew.

If there's beef, he's in the background so he doesn't start anything. He'll fight if he has to, but only after the rest of the crew decides to. He keeps quiet because he doesn't want to do anything that might start any trouble and he doesn't want to seem like a herb and say something like, "Yo, let's drop it!" And he's not a herb—he's just confused.

The Herb

He's a follower. A herb, by my definition, is someone who compromises his/her morals for the satisfaction of his friends. He does what the majority of the crew wants to do. He's the one that ends up being used, because he has no backbone. He never disagrees with whatever the rest of the crew says or does.

He never has any ideas of his own. He's afraid that if he suggests something to do, the crew will think he's a herb trying to be something he's not. For example, if most of the crew wanted to do something that this particular herb didn't feel was right, he'd do it anyway. Simply because he feels the need to be like everyone else and be accepted.

In the case of any beef, these characters are either the loud ones or overly quiet. If someone says, "Yo, $&%^* these n-ggas," the herb says, "Yo, we gonna do something or not?" If they weren't herbs, they wouldn't wait for anyone else to start something—they'd start it themselves. They always wait for somebody to speak first, to make sure they have back up.

This kind of herb makes a lot of noise when he's with his boys, but doesn't usually do it when he's alone. The beast only comes out when he's with the crew.

Shawn wrote this story when he was 19. He received a graduate degree in education and became a high school principal.

The Life and Times of a Decepticon

By David Quiles Guzman

I first encountered the Decepticons, one of New York City's most dangerous gangs, when I attended my old high school. My gym class was in the schoolyard on an ordinary cloudy day when they came into the neighborhood.

A group of about 50 youths crossed through the schoolyard chanting something, and then went back out onto the street. At first I thought it was another school coming to play us at football, but then they found their victim.

It was a young man doing repairs on an old automobile. The gang surrounded the automobile, ripped off the fender, and hit the man over the head with it. Others stomped or kicked his head while the rest did a dance on the automobile. After the gang finished, they broke up and ran their separate ways.

In Too Deep

I never saw such fear in the faces of my peers. My old high school was basically a quiet school and usually had little or no action. They looked on helplessly from the other side of the schoolyard fence.

In the following days the students were kept inside the school until the closing bell, because school officials were afraid of rumors that the Decepticons would return. Many of the students looked at their watches throughout the day, fearing that 3 o'clock would soon arrive. I could feel the tension in the air.

A few months ago, at my new school, I met Sue. Sue was once a Decepticon, but was one of the few who managed to escape the lifestyle. It was hard to believe that Sue, a sweet, generous girl, once assaulted people.

I asked her if I could interview her and she agreed, but only under the condition that her identity be closely guarded. We met a few weeks later.

"I used to hear people in the school talking about the Decepticons," she told me, "but I never knew what that was."

She stared at the top of the table where I interviewed her, as if looking through a window. She told her story without stopping.

Sue was a straight-A student at her high school, where she was fully exposed to the gang.

"There was this girl named Jackie," she continued. "She was a Deceptinet and she introduced me to all these girls who were Deceptinets.

"Jackie was always asking me to go on this 'demo' because she used to like me. One day I said, 'Yeah, I don't care,' and she told me to go to the subway station. I remember her telling me to wear jeans and sneakers, so I thought it was a party.

"I went down there to the subway station and they all separated. These two girls came up the escalator and Jackie comes up to the girl and says, 'Excuse me, but what was that you said to me the other day?' The girl was like, 'What are you talking about?' Jackie says, 'You said something to me real smart that I didn't like the other day.' So Jackie just knocked the hell out of her. All of them started rushing them and beating them up.

"We heard the cops coming and Jackie goes, 'Sue, run!' We all separated. I just couldn't believe it. They were beating the heck out of those girls."

In the weeks to come Sue became a member.

"I was glad I met these people," Sue told me. "We used to go to schools and beat people up and get paid."

Sometimes the violence would be so intense that Sue said she would "have to walk away, stand in the corner, and start crying because I couldn't believe what I was doing."

Sue's grades began to drop as she became more involved with the gang. It got to the point that she would cut every day.

One night Sue met up with Curly, another member of the gang. The gang had gone to a local high school because the school was having a party that they wanted to spoil.

> **Kids in gangs are fighting something inside of themselves—something angry. They're fighting to get attention.**

But they did little spoiling that night. Jason, the gang leader, had his head busted open in a fight.

"I was like, 'What happened?' and Curly said, 'We went down to the school and this whole football team came out on us. We was whippin' butt until a lot of those n-ggers just jetted on us. Jason got his head busted open with a chair.' Man, I was crying," Sue recalled.

"One thing about the gang is that they have a lot of heart for each other but they're fighting something inside of themselves—something angry. Decepticons are people who feel they don't have enough attention. They've been fighting so long to get attention."

inally Sue began to realize that what she was doing was wrong.

"I was getting tired of whipping people for no reason. I

wouldn't want someone to catch me sitting in the corner and start whipping on me for no reason.

"All my life was becoming Decepticons, Decepticons, and it scared me," Sue continued. "I was like, 'God, what have I gotten myself into?' I didn't know it was going to get so out of hand.

"I left the gang and stopped going to school. Because I left the gang I was afraid they would try to beat me up, so I told my father, 'Get me out of here, I got to get out of here.'

> **I was like, 'God, what have I gotten myself into?' I didn't know it was going to get so out of hand.**

"There was no way I was going to stay in New York City. My grades were down and everything," Sue said.

With help from her father, she moved out of New York and into an aunt's house in another state for the summer.

Away from the environment and influence of the gang, Sue gained self-confidence and time to grow mentally. When she returned to New York City she saw the Decepticons in a different light.

"A lot of the original members are gone. Most of them are in jail, a lot of them are dead. Some went to jail and came back a whole new person, and some got lost like me.

"A couple of weeks ago I heard Jason is sitting in the hospital saying, 'Yeah, when I get out of here I'm gonna beat up some people.' He hasn't learned his lesson," Sue said.

"Now that I'm back, my school has helped me a lot. I'm gonna be takin' college classes in February. There's nothing that can pull me down."

I wish her lots of luck.

The author was 18 when he wrote this story. He graduated from Hunter College with a degree in English.

Remembering Mike

By Carlos Lavezzari

It was in the winter, very close to Christmas. I remember coming home from a friend's house about 3:30 in the afternoon and seeing two TV news vans parked in front of my building. There were people all over the place in a frantic state. Some of my friends and neighbors were standing around, crying.

I ran up to try to get someone to tell me what had happened. No one answered me so I went inside. In the lobby all of the holiday decorations were ripped down and the Christmas tree looked as if it had been trampled.

Just then one of my friends came downstairs saying that Mike had been shot.

I couldn't believe it. I had just played basketball with Mike the day before and he was saying how one day he was going to play for the NBA. And now he was dead?

In Too Deep

I ran outside to see if it was true. I saw Mike's sister with a look on her face as if she were lost. One of my friends walked up to me and told me the first of many stories I was to hear about what had happened.

He said Mike had been in a schoolyard with a Puerto Rican girl whose brother was the local gang's leader. Mike was sitting with the girl, eating. Three members of the gang walked up and told them that they were going to tell her brother.

When the girl's brother got there, he said, "I don't want my sister round no n-ggers," and shot everyone in the park. He caught one of my friends in the leg, another in the arm, and Mike in the chest.

After hearing this I found myself wishing I had been there, thinking maybe I could have done something. Maybe I could have talked Mike into going home or been able to warn him about the type of person the girl's brother was.

I started feeling bad—bad about the fact that I never told him how thankful I was for all the times he had my back in a fight, or for letting me hide in his house when people wanted to jump me. I never got to thank him for sneaking me into his house when I ran away from home, or for being a good friend to talk to when I was feeling down.

The last thing I remember saying to him was, "See you tomorrow." "Tomorrow" was the day he died.

Now I see how life is taken for granted. Youth today are known to do that. You think because you're young you have many days to look forward to. You've got time to burn.

But that may not be true, as I have learned. If anything, this tragic happening taught me two lessons: never take people important to you for granted and never wait to tell someone just how much they mean to you. You never know when it will be your last time seeing them.

Carlos was 16 when he wrote this story.

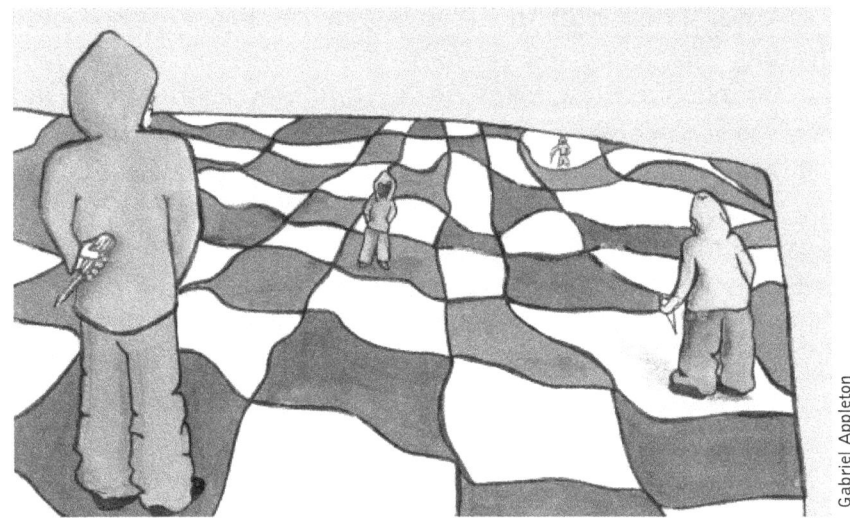

In Too Deep

By Phillip Hodge

I was in my 4th period class when a friend came in and said, "You heard about what happened outside? A kid got stabbed in the head."

I was shocked. "With a knife?" I asked.

"No, with a screwdriver," he said. I was even more shocked. Later that day, my girlfriend told me she was there and saw what happened.

"It seemed like they were play wrestling," she explained, "and then it got serious and one kid pulled out something and suddenly a screwdriver was in his head."

The kid didn't die, but he was in a coma for a long time. "How can teenagers be so evil?" I thought. "What motivates actions like that?"

Then I heard rumors that it was gang-related. For weeks last spring, students in my school were jumpy about the gang rumors. One day we were even let out an hour early, because there was a rumor that the Bloods were coming to my school to recruit.

I'm not sure how many of the rumors were true, but I did start to see people joining. Now, I know people from different gangs and they're good people, so I always wonder why they feel the need to be in a gang.

Recently I went to a teen center, where young people and adults got together to talk about teen violence and to try to answer the question, "Why do people join gangs?"

The adult speakers said that kids who join gangs are neglected at home, so they're looking for attention elsewhere. They're looking for a family outside of their own family and for protection if they need it.

The kids in the audience disagreed. They said most teens join gangs to fit in. It's just like wanting to join the popular crowd—you're looking for a place to hang and people to hang with, something to belong to, a way to feel important.

Unfortunately, gangs aren't all about hanging out as friends. They glorify violence and gang members often get in serious trouble.

At the meeting I talked to Raul Rodriguez, 19, who joined the Latin Kings when he was 16 because he wanted to be like his brother, Papo.

"He said he wanted to watch my back, so he made me join," Raul said. "I always wanted to, in a way, because some of my brother's friends were mad cool, and I used to talk with them when they were over about how it was being in the Kings."

Normally, if you want to be in the Latin Kings, you have to get "jumped in" (meaning beat up) by 10 or more people. Raul was lucky. Since his brother was already a member, they allowed him to get jumped in by three people instead.

When he joined, Raul thought his life would get a lot more exciting. "I thought I would have fights with other gangs, people watching my back all the time, and I would start staying out late," he said. When Raul got his gold and black beads, he thought he would get respect from everyone.

At first, though, nothing seemed to change. He still hung out with his old friends and was treated the same way as before.

"Papo would tell me to go home when they were about to do something," Raul said.

But after a while, other gang members would call him up to help them jump somebody. The first time he went he was nervous, but he said "it felt good at the same time" because he was eager to prove his gangsta status.

"A bunch of us went with our yellow flags and knocked on some kid's door. His mother answered and my boy asked for Sean. When he came out, we all jumped him," said Raul.

The kid's mother called the cops, but everyone had already left by the time they came.

Being in the gang never got Raul in trouble with the cops, but it caused problems at home. When Raul's mother found out, she told him to quit or to move out. She didn't want him to get in trouble.

When Raul got his gold and black beads, he thought he would get respect from everyone.

Raul thought it was unfair that she had left Papo alone when he joined a gang, so he moved in with a friend for a few weeks. When he came back, his mother wouldn't speak to him.

Eventually, after his brother was put in jail for selling drugs, Raul quit the gang. He decided to stop because he didn't want to wind up the same way. "If I stayed I would have winded up selling, getting in trouble for something stupid," he said.

Plus, his sister had a baby, and Raul didn't want to set a negative example for his nephew. Now that he's not a King, his mother has started talking to him again, too.

But not everyone gets out before they get in trouble.

In Too Deep

Izzy, 16, who has been a member of the Bloods for three years, wound up in jail for 10 months for doing what he called "foolish things." Now part of a program called City Challenge, Izzy is changing his life around.

Izzy said he joined the gang because he was a quiet kid who wanted to fit in with the popular crowd in his school, and the popular kids were in gangs.

"I was going with the in-crowd. Me personally, I'm not the violent type," Izzy said. Some friends of his asked Izzy to join, and at first he didn't think it was a good idea. He wondered, "What would my mom think? What would be the outcome of joining the gang?"

But when Izzy started seeing the gang expanding, he didn't want to feel left out—so he decided to join, even though his mother was his role model and he knew she would be hurt.

After a while, his mother found out from other people in the neighborhood that he was in the gang, and they got in a big fight. "She didn't really disown me, but she didn't really think it was me," Izzy said quietly.

Izzy was looking for close friendship, but that's not what he got.

"I thought it was gonna be some type of unity and I found out it was something different," he said. "I would see them in the street and say, 'What's up?' But me chillin' with them, them being really friendly—it wasn't like that."

Last year, Izzy got in trouble with the law and was sent upstate to a boot-camp style prison for 10 months. Because he was doing well in the program, Izzy was made a teen leader in a group where cadets talked through their problems. Many of the other teens had been locked up for several years, and in the group they talked about how they would feel going home, and what sorts of family issues they had dealt with when they were younger.

By helping others, Izzy also learned to solve his own problems. "I had issues and I shared my issues and I got feedback, and they shared and I gave feedback. It was one hand washing another," he said.

When Izzy was in the boot camp, he started to feel confident about himself and to believe he could aspire to more than the thug life. And when adults saw how he had begun to change, they helped him out.

Izzy said the staff at City Challenge have given him their home phone numbers and been available to talk to him whenever he needed someone to listen.

Izzy joined the gang because he wanted to fit in with the popular crowd in his school, and the popular kids were in gangs.

"I had a lot of family support and would come to City Challenge whenever I have problems. I was always to myself and now I'm more open. It's made me strong mentally," he said. "Kids should be able to open up to older role models. It's good to find someone doing the right thing, something that's positive."

With help from a mentor at City Challenge, Izzy ended up getting a basketball scholarship to play for a private school. He hopes that he will be able to go to college on scholarship.

Izzy said going to school outside the city has changed his life. "It got me away from gangs and it's a lot different," he said. "I get more help in private school, it's friendlier. The people congratulate you on your efforts, the things you do."

Izzy is also in the process of getting out of the Bloods. "I've got a lot of opportunities playing ball and going to school and I feel I shouldn't have to be inside a gang," he said.

A lot of kids like Izzy and Raul join gangs just because they are looking for friends and acceptance. They don't think they can find that unless they join a gang. But, like Izzy, many teens who join gangs might feel better about themselves if they were involved in more positive groups.

In Too Deep

There are a lot of different organizations out there for youth who have positive motives, but it's harder to find out about positive groups than to join a gang. Besides, people don't want to be seen as punks.

Too many people seem to think it's good living in the ghetto, not heading anywhere, staying poor, and hanging out drinking and getting into trouble. I'm not against hanging out or drinking, but take it from Izzy and Raul: if that's what you live for, you're not going far.

Phillip wrote this story when he was 19.

The Last to Know

By Anonymous

When I first started talking to Jay online a year ago, he seemed just like every other boy: He talked to a million different girls on MySpace and he told half of them that he would date them at the same time. I felt that he was trying to be a player to boost his ego, and that was a turnoff to me.

But I fell for his humor after talking to him every day for a month. We'd spend the whole night chatting online, cracking jokes about each other. After all the hostility I had for him faded, I saw who he was. He spoke very well and over the phone he'd compliment me and open up to me about how he felt.

I told him I didn't want him to say "I love you" to the other girls online or try to meet up with them. He agreed, and I trusted him. After two months, he asked me out and I accepted. I thought being in a relationship with such a good-natured guy would be easy.

But a few weeks later, Jay called one night and told me he'd cut his arm in a fight after a bunch of guys jumped him and his friends. This was the first I'd heard of him fighting, and I was so upset I cried. The way his friends dressed in pictures he'd shown me and the things they wrote on his MySpace page made me assume they were thugs. I had a feeling they might lead him into trouble and next time he wouldn't be as lucky as he'd been that night. I made him swear to me that he wouldn't fight again. He agreed with no hesitation.

Then he said something that got my full attention: "Would you mind if I became a Crip?"

Still, after that I started to worry about the type of people he hung out with. I'd noticed a sudden change in Jay when he was around one of his friends, Keith. He spoke louder and used more slang when Keith was there. Even worse, when I was with just Jay and Keith, they forgot I existed. I hadn't expected Jay to leave me to one side for his friend, and it made me worry about the influences his friends had over him. I talked to him about how I felt when he left me out, and after that Jay tried to include me in conversations more. For a long time, everything seemed OK.

Then, almost a year later, I was hanging out at Jay's house when Keith walked in. Jay paused his video game because Keith started to tell a story of a fight that had gone down in the park a few blocks from his house.

I lay there just listening as the boys went through an exchange of "word"s and "a'ight"s. They seemed to get more excited about every new detail: the punches that were thrown, who did it, who got a track ripped out of their hair.

Keith finished with, "You should have been there."

"I was with my beautiful girlfriend," Jay replied, taking a glance back at me and kissing my forehead.

"You could have brought her, the girls were fighting too,"

Keith said with a shrug.

My eyebrows shot up. "I would have run the other way!"

"That's messed up," both boys said.

"You would have left with me. You know I don't like you fighting," I told Jay.

"Of course, baby," he answered with a smile.

This was the first time I found out for certain that two of Jay's best friends were in gangs. And Jay was so into Keith's story that I started to wonder how much—or how little—it would take for his friends to persuade him to do the things I'd asked him not to do. Though I told myself he was being honest with me, I began to wonder if he just said he wouldn't fight when I was there.

About two months passed. Then one night I woke up to my phone ringing at about 1:30 a.m. I answered and heard my boyfriend's voice on the other end. He seemed to be wide awake, but I was so tired I was hardly listening to what he was saying.

Then he said something that got my full attention: "Would you mind if I became a Crip?"

I thought I was hearing things so I answered, "Huh?"

"Nothing," he replied.

I felt panic fluttering around in my stomach. "Don't do that. Seriously, that would be stupid," I said.

After that he started to talk about something else, the conversation ended and we hung up. I tried not to stress myself about it. I knew many girls who didn't care that their boyfriends were in gangs. I didn't want to care, either. I felt not caring would be easier on me and would save a lot of stress on the relationship.

But it did bother me. When I spoke to him early the next morning, I asked him what he'd meant by that question. He told me that he didn't remember asking it. I didn't believe him, but it was so early I didn't feel like arguing, so I just let it pass by.

One day about a month later, I was instant messaging one of my newest friends, Selma, who was also the girlfriend of my boyfriend's best friend, Gavin. Gavin was in the gang. On this day, she was telling me about an argument they'd had and her frustration about him still being in a gang. I told her that I told my boyfriend not to go into that, and how I was glad that wasn't one of our problems. Then she told me something that I would never forget.

"He started two months ago," she wrote to me.

I felt my blood grow warm. I knew she was wondering why I didn't know and I felt embarrassed. I felt absolutely blind-sided.

> **I knew many girls who didn't care that their boyfriends were in gangs. I didn't want to care, either.**

A few minutes later, I called Jay. I was so furious that I didn't say a word for a long time.

"Did you join that gang?" I asked finally.

He was quiet for a while. "Why do you ask? Who said something to you?"

I told him that my friend had told me and I just needed to hear it from him. I wanted him to tell me that it wasn't true. When he confessed, I felt more hurt. I yelled at him, saying this didn't affect just him; if someone doesn't like him, they could easily hurt someone he loves. He told me that he didn't know how to tell me, that he didn't want to disappoint me.

"But why did you join?" I yelled.

"When I was out with my friends who'd joined the gang, I'd see people I'd known before my friends knew them, but they would notice my friends first," he said. "Many times they wouldn't acknowledge me at all. Now that I'm in it, everyone knows me. Even people I don't know, know my name."

When he explained this to me, it didn't surprise me. I'd begun to notice after we'd been together a few months that he was different from me in one major respect. I like to live in the shadows and don't like feeling that everyone knows everything about me, but he likes attention and the center stage.

Even though I'd noticed this about him, I felt confused when he told me he'd joined the gang so he'd be known. He has always been the one to say to me, "Don't listen to what people say." It stuck with me. But he didn't take his own advice, and that was disappointing. For a whole week I was spiteful toward him. But when I thought things over, I felt this was probably a phase he would get over soon. I also felt guilty about pushing him away after I found out. I felt I should support him in his biggest decisions. He had always listened to my problems and helped me get through the worst days.

Eventually, I calmed down. I did have trouble trusting him, because he hid what he'd done from me for so long. But looking back, I think he probably worried about how to tell me, because he knew how I might react.

After I found out, he told me that he wanted to keep the gang separate from his relationship with me so that I wouldn't know about what he was doing and worry. That made me worry more, though, because if something happened I wouldn't know or be able to help at all. I didn't tell him that, because I knew that he wants to feel he can handle things on his own. I accept this and just try to be a person he can come to if he wants to get away from the gang scene for a while.

Now it's several months later, and I really don't hear anything about him being in the gang. If I want to know something, I have to ask him. I feel a bit relieved that he doesn't seem to be too active in the gang, but I still want him to quit. If he doesn't get out of it in a year or so, I will reconsider building a future with him like we've been planning, because that's not something I would want to be around for the rest of my life. If we were to have a family together, I would not want that kind of lifestyle shown to my children or passed along to them.

I think gangs are for men who like being out on the streets because they think they are too good for following rules, wearing a suit, getting up in the morning and having a boss. But men who have drive to do something more productive with their lives realize they can use their abilities and have something to show for their lives.

I believe Jay has the drive to be someone great in this world because he is a talented artist. He told me that he wants to go forward with his dream of being an animator and I am always pushing him to do all he can to make it happen. He still makes me happy and makes me laugh. So for now, I deal with my worrying and anger by hoping that in the end, he'll see the gang isn't making him better. As he starts to see his fellow gang members go nowhere, I hope he'll push himself to do better.

The author was 17 when she wrote this story.

Almost One of the Gang

By Anonymous

When I was in 8th grade, all my friends started joining the Crips gang. They bragged about how cool they were, and they made gang life look so easy and fun. I hung out with them to learn more and just to be able to say I hung out with gang members. I liked being friends with them—for protection and to be cool. But I also made sure I didn't join the gang.

I realized what my friends were and what I was not. They'd been brought up in environments where they had to be in a gang to survive. I grew up in a good home with my mom and brother, and I'd encountered fewer obstacles than they had. Though I wondered what it would be like to be in a gang, I knew I couldn't handle gang life. Some of the things gangs did, like robbery, murders and hustling, just weren't for me.

None of my friends ever directly approached me about joining because I always told them that hanging out with them was as far as I would go. My friends respected my refusal to join because, except for actually being in the gang, I fit right in with them. I even fought with them whenever they got into a beef, so they knew I was a real friend and not just a tag-along. For a little while I worried I was in too deep, fighting with the Crips against rival gangs, but I was careful not to go any further than that.

Now I'm a junior in high school and I'm still friends with gang members. I'm comfortable with my role and my friends are too, so I don't face much pressure to join. But I see a lot of my classmates being pressured in my high school. I see blue bandannas, the color of the Crips, all the time in my school. I see blue beads around people's wrists and necks and the letter C (for Crips) thrown up in every direction in the hallways.

Almost everybody in my school has some kind of gang affiliation, even the security guards. Many of the guards are Crips and they greet students who are gang members by "piecing" them (doing the gang handshake). They even yell out the Crips calls, like "Co-rip" and "Blat killa" (a dis to the Bloods, a rival gang).

Usually the Crips and the Bloods hang out together at my school, and they don't have problems with each other. This is common in a lot of high schools, according to my friends who are gang members. Even though the gangs are sworn enemies, they're usually about peace in the school building. They have the occasional rumble in the hallway, but for the most part they get along.

But that doesn't mean there isn't violence. One day during my sophomore year, a freshman named Kellz transferred in from another school. When Kellz noticed that our school was mainly Crips territory, he foolishly pretended to be a Crip.

A week after Kellz came, a Crip named Speed asked him what set he was with. A set is a division of a gang based on neighborhood or street, sort of like precincts to the police. They were in the lunchroom, and I joined the crowd of students that had started to build around them.

Kellz answered, "Original Gangsta Crip" and it just so happened that was Speed's set. Speed immediately knew he was lying. Kellz tried to apologize, but to no avail. He was so scared I could see it in his face.

Then it got even crazier. The whole time he'd been claiming to be a Crip, he was actually a Blood. We found out when somebody from his neighborhood said they'd seen him around with the Bloods. The Bloods didn't take too kindly to the news either. Eventually almost every gang member in the school pummeled him. The Crips beat him up for pretending to be a Crip, and the Bloods beat him up for being afraid to admit he was a Blood.

> **The Crips beat him up for pretending to be a Crip, and the Bloods beat him up for being afraid to admit he was a Blood.**

That reassured me that I'd made the right decision not to join a gang. But what made me even more sure that gang life wasn't for me was when I witnessed my first and last initiation for a new Crips member.

One day last year, I was walking with some Crip friends and they told me they were about to square somebody in. I didn't know what that meant. My friend explained that it's when the gang recruits a new member by beating him down to make him prove he's strong enough to be in the gang.

There was a dead end behind the park where the new recruit, Ramon, met up with the Crips to be squared in. I was cool with Ramon, and I decided to watch to see how it worked.

First Ramon fought one of my homeboys for 20 seconds. Twenty seconds later, another gang member joined, and then another every 20 seconds after that. The rule was that if Ramon fell to his knees at any point, he'd have to start all over with the first guy.

Soon there were three guys fighting Ramon at once. I could hear each blow connecting to various parts of his body, the worst of them on his head. Eventually he fell to the ground in the fetal position, blood all over his face. He hadn't even made it to the fourth gang member, so they didn't bother to pick him up and start over. They just began stomping on his head and all over his body.

Even more terrifying were the looks on the faces of the Crips as they beat him senseless. They were smiling and laughing like it was funny. They seemed to be enjoying it. "Get the hell up!" they yelled at him as he fell. One of the boys beating him senseless was his brother.

When it was all said and done, the gang members tried to help Ramon up, but he kept falling. While they waited for him to get himself together, they congratulated each other and talked about who beat him the worst.

Ramon finally got up and they all congratulated him for fighting his best and told him that he was down with them. He couldn't even talk. I left after that and all I could do was think about it for the rest of the night. Any thoughts I'd had of joining a gang died then and there. I was so glad that I'd had the presence of mind to not join.

> **My friend Mike told me he became a Crip because his whole block and neighborhood pressured him.**

The next week, Ramon came to school showing off his new lifestyle. He wouldn't stop talking about it, and he was walking around like nobody could touch him. It was as if he didn't even remember what had happened to him the week before. After that, he started hanging out with the cool kids and getting into fights, and people respected him.

From what I see from my friends, the main reason they turn to gang life is peer pressure. I think Ramon joined because he didn't want to disappoint his friends. It can be hard to say no to people you've known your whole life. My friend Mike told me he became a Crip because his whole block and neighborhood pressured him. He also told me he felt uncomfortable by himself and wanted protection.

I understand wanting people to protect you just in case you need some help, but I don't know if joining a gang makes anything better. Once you're in one, you probably need even more protection than you did before.

I still spend most of my time with friends who are in gangs. I know there's a pretty fine line between hanging out with a gang and joining one. But it's a line I've made clear to myself and my friends, and I'm not going to cross it.

The author was in high school when he wrote this story.

My Crew Was My Family

By Xavier Reyes

I ran away on the day my adoptive mother found out I had stolen $1,200 from her. I had stolen the money over a period of six months, but by the time she found out I had already spent it all. I knew I had to run away because she was about to go off on me.

When she put me on the back porch (like she always did, whenever she got mad at me) and went to call the cops, I had my opportunity. I grabbed a shirt off the clothesline and a pair of socks. Then I picked up a pair of rubber duckies (rain shoes) and jumped over my next door neighbor's fence.

At first I didn't know where I was going. Then I decided to go to the movies like I always did when I ran away. I had no money, so I snuck in through a side door. I saw *Robin Hood: Prince of Thieves* and then left.

It was 5 p.m. by that time and I was getting hungry, so I

decided to go to Key Food and help people with their grocery bags. I stayed for two hours. I would have stayed longer, but I knew I had to keep moving. From what, I had no idea.

My first night in the streets was horrible. I slept in the bushes by the church, down the block from where my mother lived. I couldn't sleep that well because I had to keep one eye open to make sure that nobody saw me.

For the first few weeks in the streets it was the same thing over and over. Sneaking in the movies, then bagging groceries to make money, then going to sleep with one eye open.

After the third week I knew I had to move somewhere else because things were getting too quiet. I thought about the beach. Since it was the summer, it would be hard for people to find me in a place that was crowded during the day and dark as hell at night.

The first couple of days at the beach were very good. During the day I would help the fishermen by running to get coffee and donuts for them. At night I would go on the piers and watch people catch crabs. Whenever I got tired, I would go and sleep under the boardwalk.

I stayed at the beach for two weeks. Then I left because I thought I saw my mother there one day.

My next home was in a bunch of bushes in the projects on Nostrand Ave. It was a good place to hide because they were very thick and it was impossible for anybody to see me.

Once I crawled inside, I was concealed from the rest of the world. I never got wet when it rained because I put an old shower curtain on top of the bushes and wore my rubber duckies and raincoat. The only real problem I had was when the ground became muddy. Then I would wind up in the nearest bathroom washing myself longer than usual.

One day when I was bagging groceries at Key Food, this girl came up to me with her friend and asked me if I had a few bucks so she could buy a forty. To be honest with you, I didn't know what the hell a forty was, but I told her to come back in 15 minutes because I didn't have the money. She said OK and left.

Fifteen minutes later she came back by herself. She asked me if I had the money. I said yeah and gave it to her, then she left. About 20 minutes later she came back and asked me if I wanted to come and chill with her for a while. I said yeah.

> **There was no one to tell me what to do or where to go. I was running with a gang and doing my thing.**

When we left the store, she started to ask me questions about where I lived and what my name was. I gave her my real name but a fake address. She told me her name was Lisa, but that her crew called her Dimples. Then she asked me if I wanted to hang out with her crew. Not knowing any better, I said yeah.

We walked to the corner and sat down. After two minutes of silence, a whole bunch of guys came from the opposite corner. They came toward us with a somewhat arrogant walk. They got closer to us and I started to get nervous. When they got two feet away from us the skinniest one said:

"Dimples, what's up?"

"Nothing, what's up with y'all?"

"We chilling. Who's the kid?"

When he said that I looked away, scared of what might happen.

"He cool, he cool."

That made me turn my head back.

"Whatcha mean?" said a guy with a bald head.

"Exactly what I mean. He cool!"

"So you saying Shorty going to be down with us?" another guy said, who looked half white and half Puerto Rican.

"Yeah."

Someone from behind the crowd yelled, "Aw, Shorty down

with the crew!"

"Yes, Shorty!" someone else screamed.

Then they all came towards me and I stood up. One by one they gave me a pound and told me their tags.

"Whuz up, I'm Sprite."

"Photo."

"N.W.A.P." (Which stood for N-gga With A Problem.)

"Guess Man."

"Yeah, whuz up, I'm Smiley."

About 15 of them told me their tags. It was a mixed posse: whites, blacks, and Puerto Ricans. I thought I was so cool. I thought that I was finally going to be who I really wanted to be. But little did I know what that was.

Life was a breeze for me. There was no one to tell me what to do or where to go. I was running with a gang and doing my thing. Sometimes I would wonder what my adoptive mother was doing back home. Was she crying, laughing, dying, or surviving?

All of a sudden I'd stop and remember that she was the reason I was in the streets. When I lived at home, she would physically abuse me and treat me differently from her biological children. Now I didn't need her or her family because I had my crew. My crew was my family.

When I first became part of the crew, I didn't know anything about drinking beer or smoking buddah. The thing that I did know was how to survive on my own.

My first blunt came to me as a surprise.

"Here Shorty."

"What's this?"

"A blunt."

"Oh damn!"

"What?"

"Nothing, it's just that I ain't never smoked one before."

"You for real?"

"Hell yeah."

"OK, this is between me and you only."

"Yeah."

"You hold it and take a pull like this."

Mike took the blunt from me, then put it to his lips and took a loooong pull. He held the smoke for about 10 seconds, then let it out.

"So that's how you do it!"

"Yup, ain't nothing to it. Here, you try."

I took the blunt and did the same thing he did—took a pull, held it in for 10 seconds, and then let it out. The smoke burned my throat and I started coughing.

"Easy, Shorty, easy."

"Damn, what the hell you trying to do? Kill me?"

"If you weren't going so damn fast, maybe you wouldn't have coughed."

"Fast? Then why don't you show me how damn fast or slow to go?"

"Here, now watch me very closely."

He took the blunt from me and did the same thing he had done before. Then he handed it back to me.

"You see, you got to have finesse. Don't rush, but don't take your time. You'll get the hang of it. Here, try again."

I took the blunt from him and took another pull. Not too fast, not too slow. When I finished blowing out the smoke I handed it back to him. This time I didn't cough or choke. Although it burned my throat, I didn't show it.

"You see, now you got the hang of it."

He gave me a pound and we both finished off the rest of the blunt. Once in a while I coughed, but then I would stop immediately.

By the time we finished I thought I was in a different world. When I stood up I broke out laughing. I don't know why, but I did. I kept laughing for a half hour. Then I had to stop because my stomach started to hurt me. The only thing that Mark did was just sit there looking as stupid as he was.

When I had my first bit of weed is when things began to change for me. I finally had a chance to escape and go on my own little adventure. Whenever things got bad for me, all I did was gather up some money to buy a fat Philly and my problems were gone.

Or at least I thought they were.

Day after day I hung out with my crew. When they went home, I went to make some money. By the time we met again I usually had enough to buy two nickel bags or a dime bag.

The sorrow I felt for my adoptive mother and family was no longer present. A feeling of hatred took its place.

After the weed came the beer. If I drank a forty and smoked a blunt afterwards, I would be messed up! I would do that almost every day. I was becoming an alcoholic and a drug addict and I was only 13 years old!

Things were fine for a while until I went back to my original hobby. Stealing. To be honest with you, I used to love stealing. It was the main thing I was good at.

I used to steal anything from clothes to food. Sometimes me and the crew would go out together and bumrush stores. Since I was the smallest but quickest one, I usually came out with the most stuff. Stealing was the main way that I got clothes when I was on the street.

When my crew began to notice that I was a near expert at stealing, they decided to show me how to steal something bigger and much more valuable. Never in my wildest dreams had I dreamed about stealing a car.

That night when we got ready to leave I thought about not going. But Guess Man talked me into it. On the way, they gave me a few pointers.

In Too Deep

"When you're popping the steering column, try to cut down on the noise."

"Since you are the lookout person, whenever you see somebody coming, knock on the car once and walk away, then come back in five minutes. Got it?"

"Yeah, got it."

"Okay, let's do it!"

We walked for about 45 minutes until Photo stopped in front of a Lincoln Town Car.

"This is the one we want. Right N.W.A.P.?"

"Hell yeah!"

"Let's get to work."

Photo and N.W.A.P. got in the car. Mark, Smiley, and me stood by the car, while Sprite and Reggie waited on the corners. They wanted to make sure that the cops wouldn't pull up on us.

Then we started. I glimpsed into the car and saw N.W.A.P. and Photo trying to pop the steering column. After about three minutes of noise they got the car started.

Photo rolled down the window and told us to hop in. I was so scared I was shivering. Me, Mark, and Smiley hopped into the back seat. We went to the corner and got Sprite and Reggie, and off we went to steal another one.

After we stole our second car of the night we went to a big field across from Marine Park and played Crash-A-Derby. The way you play it is by crashing the cars while you're driving around in a circle. After we finished, the car doors were smashed in, the front hood was part of the windshield, and they were stuck together like Siamese twins (kids, please don't try this at home).

We finished our fun at about 3 o'clock in the morning, and unfortunately we had to walk back. Afterwards we went to the store and bought cigarettes and beer. We chilled until about 6 a.m., then we split up and went our separate ways.

As I was walking back to my hiding place in the bushes, I started to think about life, and why my life had turned out the way it was. I knew it was my mother's fault, but it wasn't fun being a criminal. That was the only thing I was experienced in doing. Stealing, drinking and smoking were three of my favorite things on the streets. I was just another problem that society couldn't handle. I knew I had to change my lifestyle, but I didn't know how or where to begin.

The summer was coming to an end and my crew had to get ready to go back to school. Most of them had gotten left back the year before, so this year they had to do good or else their moms would kick them out the house.

There were times that they used to ask me what school I was going to. I would tell them that I wasn't sure yet and immediately change the subject.

When school did start, my peeps had mad new clothes. I wanted new clothes too, but new clothes don't last when you're on the run. On the run from the truth—the truth that I had made my life the way it was and I was the only one who could change it.

Day after day I would watch my friends go to school and get an education. The only thing I was doing was making money for weed and beer.

On Saturday my crew and I would stay out late, but on Sunday nights the crew had to go in early because they had to go to school. When they went in I would stay out later, just hoping the 5-0's wouldn't catch me.

Every day I got more and more depressed. I needed someone to show me the right way. I needed someone to care for me and to love me. I needed someone to tell me who I really was.

Three weeks after school started my crew was chilling on a Sunday night. It was still early, 9:30 p.m. Then for some strange reason they kept on asking me when was I going to go home. I kept telling them that I couldn't, because my mother wasn't home yet.

By 10:30 Lisa and Photo said they would walk me home. They said it in such a way that I couldn't use the excuse, "My mother isn't home" anymore. So I said peace to the rest of the crew and we began walking.

"So, Shorty, what does your mom do?" Photo asked.

"She's a nurse."

"Really!" Lisa asked, sounding surprised.

"Yeah really," I said.

We made a left turn onto the block where I told them I lived, although I really didn't. I was starting to get nervous.

"Do you think she's home now?" Photo asked, looking down the dark block, then turning to me.

"Nah."

"Is anybody home?" Lisa then asked, while lighting up a cigarette.

Oh &#%*^, I thought to myself, I think that they know. What do I do? Do I run? Nah, can't do that, 'cause Photo with his speedy Gonzalez butt would probably catch me.

"Huh?" Lisa asked again, breaking into my thoughts.

"Na, na, nobody home," I said.

We kept walking down the block until I stopped at a house with a white iron fence and no car in front. I told Lisa and Photo to go wait down the block until I waved, because I didn't want my neighbors to tell my mother that they saw me coming home with a bunch of kids.

They walked down the block and stopped. I turned towards the front door and pretended to knock on it. Then I stepped inside the doorway and waved, but then instead of them walking away they walked towards me. When they got about 10 feet away, they began to talk.

"Xavier, we know about it," Lisa said.

"Know about what?" I said, walking closer to them.

"You know," Photo said.

The jig was up. They knew about it, but I tried to play it off.

"Know what," I asked again, trying to sound more serious.

"Know that you ran away from home," Lisa said, lighting up another cigarette. It began to drizzle.

"But how do y'all know?" I asked again, almost crying, but trying not to.

"Sprite."

"Sprite what?" I asked, cutting off Photo.

"Sprite followed you home the night that you and him went out to steal cars. He saw you go in the bushes in the projects on Nostrand Ave.," Lisa said.

"Damn it, damn it, damn it," I said. It was finally over. My dream life had come to an end.

"I also knew," Photo replied, and we started to walk again.

"And how did you know?" I said.

"I knew because I did the same thing you did when I was your age!" he said, almost yelling.

Then Lisa said, "You wanna talk about it?"

We walked towards the park and sat down on the table. There was no longer a drizzle. I began talking.

"I ran away from my house three months ago because I had stole $1200 from my adoptive mother. I've been living on the streets. For money I've been working in Key Food. You know, helping people with their bags and stuff like that. Please don't turn me in!"

"We have no choice," Lisa said. "Sprite talked to a guy he knows who is becoming a cop. The cop said that we would have to turn you in, or else we'd get arrested."

That was it. I couldn't let my crew get arrested, so I let them turn me in. They called up the rest of the crew and we met at the police station. When they took me in, the cop at the front desk said that there was no record of me being missing, but they took me anyway.

The first thing the cops did was ask me a whole bunch of questions, such as "How long were you on the streets?," "Where does your mother live?," and "Why did you run away?" Then he gave me some donuts with an orange soda. I asked him if I could see my friends.

He said that I could, but not to go far because a police car was coming to pick me up to take me to a shelter. I walked out of his office and back into the waiting room. Nobody in the crew was talking.

"I guess this is goodbye," I said, trying to put on a smile.

They all got up and one by one they gave me a pound, along with some advice.

"Yo Shorty, take care of yourself," Photo said, while handing me two $20 bills. I put the money in my pocket and gave him a pound.

"Shorty, I'm going to miss you. Don't forget to call us," Mark said, while handing me a piece of paper with everyone's number on it.

I knew I had to change my lifestyle, but I didn't know how or where to begin.

"Don't mess up. You don't want to end up six feet deep," N.W.A.P. said.

When it was Lisa's turn, she didn't give me a pound or advice. She gave me something I had always wanted—a nice long hug. A hug that I always will remember.

Then a tall Black cop came in and told me it was time to go. I gave everybody one last pound and walked outside. A cop held the door open for me.

When I got in the cop car, I looked out the window. Lisa and the crew had their heads down. Both cops got into the car and slammed the doors behind them. I looked out again. Their heads were up. As the car slowly pulled away, I put up the peace sign and turned ahead.

It took an hour to get to the shelter. But in that one hour I thought about my life. I knew I had to change it.

I had already learned the first step. I had to stop running. It wasn't my mother or my problems that I was running from. It was myself.

After I went into the shelter, I was placed in the system. Now I'm in a group home and I've turned my life around.

I dedicate this story to my crew, who understood somebody I didn't know—Me.

Xavier wrote this story when he was 17. He graduated from college with a degree in public affairs, and went on to work at a major media company.

When Things Get Hectic

By Juan Azize

Last summer I was headed to the bodega around my block to get a sandwich when I saw my boy Deps step to some kid I'd never seen before. Being the nosy friend that I am, I went over to see what the problem was. "Yo Deps, what's going on man?" I said.

"This punk got an eye problem," Deps answered.

"Whatever man," said the kid who was staring at Deps. I noticed he got scared when I came over, knowing there were two of us now and this wasn't his neighborhood.

But fighting over a bad look wasn't exactly the move. "Yo, forget about that man," I said. "He don't want no beef."

"So why he trying to scope if he don't want none?" said Deps.

"I wasn't scoping at you man," answered the kid.

"Yo man, squash this bullsh-t already so I could get my sandwich," I told Deps. "My stomach is growling."

"Aaiight man, just don't be trying to act like you represent around here," Deps told the kid. They both gave each other the hand along with dirty looks and slow moves.

After the fake pound, I went inside the store to get my salami and cheese and Deps tagged along. About 15 minutes later there we were chilling in front of my house. It was really hot and we were trying to throw girls in front of the hydrant and munching down that delicious sandwich when, all of a sudden, a blue Corolla with tinted windows rolled up in front of us.

I knew right away this was the kid Deps was riffing to. I remember the sandwich losing its delicious taste. The girls were still teasing us, trying to get us to chase them, when Deps tapped my leg 'cause he knew what time it was. Before I could yell "duck," I saw the back window roll down enough for a gun to fit through. I grabbed Deps like a reflex and we both hit the floor at the same time two bullets hit the side of my house.

When the weekends come in my neighborhood, I feel like I'm in a battle zone.

The car was long gone before me and Deps had a chance to feel burnt. All of a sudden the girls didn't want to play anymore and it wasn't that sunny. I never knew things could get to that point so fast. A dirty look setting bullets off didn't make any sense. What if they had caught us from behind? What if they had shot one of the girls? What if my mother had been standing there?

It really made me think deep. I wanted to kill those guys, I was so steamed. I was confused. I was flipping. I rode around with my friends looking for that blue Corolla for that whole week. Deps got a gun that same day, hoping they were going to come back (which didn't happen).

This kind of thing goes on all the time: "Yo, you heard who got shot?" "I ran into some beef today." "Yo man, bring a shank just in case." I am sick and tired of hearing it. Violence surrounds us everywhere: school, work, even in front of your crib. Kids nowadays are ready to kill each other over the dumbest things.

I know a lot of kids who are scared one day they are just going to get blasted for something stupid like that. There are so many other kids out there with guns, knives, and short tempers.

When the weekends come in my neighborhood, I feel like I'm in a battle zone. Before trooping it out to a jam I always have to make sure I'm rolling with my little crew in case things get hectic. Most of the jams I've been to end up with a shootout or a rumble.

> **It started to get hectic—people were getting shanked up and hammered down.**

And this stuff doesn't just go down where I live. In school all the gossip in the hallway is about things happening in the streets. I know lots of people also carry weapons to school but the beef is outside most of the time.

There was this time, last year in my old school, when my boy Duzer was supposed to shoot a fair one with another kid in school, so my little crew got together to keep it a fair fight.

When eighth period came we all hit the handball courts. While Duzer hopped around to get ready, I saw kids pulling shanks and hammers out of their knapsacks. I knew this wasn't going to be no fair fight. Fake gangstas try to find the easy way out.

It started to get hectic—people were getting shanked up and hammered down. I played it safe and took them sucker punches every chance I had. It was an even rumble, not counting the fact that they had more weapons. (I admit I was scared to death about them hammers.)

When the 5-0's rolled up we were gone with the wind. A couple of kids couldn't run so they stayed on the floor covering their sore spots. My boy Eliester had a thin slice on his neck and had to get 11 stitches. The rest of us had shanked jackets and arms, nothing serious (thank God).

We ran to the hospital about 10 blocks away. About a half hour later, after the hype went down, I stopped Duzer in the waiting room and asked him what the beef was all about. I almost started to laugh when I heard the answer: "He was trying to tell me who I wasn't allowed to talk to," answered Duzer. "Yo, I was up on that girl way before that n-gga even dreamed about it."

A girl! I didn't understand. One of our boys gets sliced in the neck with 11 stitches and three other kids were left on the floor bleeding like cold. This was pathetic, killing each other over a girl who's probably ready to move on to the next man. Eight tracks make better sense than that.

I'm not gonna front, though. If my boys get into more senseless beef, I'm still going to catch their backs and I won't stop to ask them what the problem is. Adrenalin flows faster than questions, and my boys have always been there for me when I needed them, without asking questions and trying to talk it out.

I guess it must be written in that invisible book that knows everything, the one where ladies go first and actions speak louder than words. The funny thing is, I follow that book. If my boys have beef again, I'll be there asking mute questions that come out too late. It's like a reflex. It shouldn't be, but it is. Your boys are your boys.

I do stop to think about it, but only after it's too late, after the damage is already done.

Juan wrote this story when he was 17.

True Love Won't Die

By Betty Dominguez

I never thought that Frank and I would ever be apart. Sure, we had that weird puppy love relationship. We used to fight and break up at least three times a day, but we couldn't live without each other. Little did I know that one day I would literally be forced to live without him. Now I wish I could still be screaming my lungs out and calling him "stupid."

I first saw Frank at a party I went to with my sister. It was a hot August night. I was not in the mood to talk to anybody. "Boring," I told my sister about the party. But she pointed to Frank and said, "He's cute." I didn't even bother to look. "Oh, please," I said. "Let's go."

One day at school in September I was feeling jumpy because a guy was staring at me. His friend came over and said, "My boy wants to talk to you." I went over and we started talking. It was

Frank. He was cool, but I was not looking for someone.

In November I decided to give him a chance. He turned out to be the sweetest thing. We would walk to class together, holding hands. He told me about the night of the party, how I never even noticed him.

By month two, I was "in love" or in what I believed was love. I needed to feel loved, and Frank made me feel that way. By month three, the fighting started.

"Don't go out."

"What are you doing, talking to him/her?"

I used to cry a lot, 'cause we'd break up so much. I needed him too much. I couldn't afford to lose him. Frank was all I had.

He was not a bad kid, but he joined a gang to be down. And even though I was against it, because I loved Frank I soon followed.

I started doing things that I usually wouldn't do before. I started cutting school and fighting. I would lie to my family. I had to go to gang meetings, so I told my family I had to go to the library. I had to fight people who never did anything wrong to me. I got used to being violent.

I was in a high gang position. This meant that I was respected—or rather feared—by everyone. And I was Frank's "wife." I felt like I belonged.

I was going to meet Frank at 4 p.m. at the subway station, but I got there an hour early. I felt like something was going to happen.

After a few months, I felt like I couldn't live without Frank or the gang. I was caught up in a world of violence, but we were a family. They gave me the love I was looking for.

A new school year was starting. I couldn't wait. Frank and I had made it through a year. We were so happy, we even thought about getting married. He once told me that he wanted me to be the mother of his first child, but he never pushed me into having sex. We never did anything more than kissing and he never made me feel bad that I was afraid to have sex. He was willing to wait until I was ready.

Frank saw other people while he was with me. Every time I found out or he'd tell me himself, he would bring her up to my face and break up with her.

But one time he broke up with me and swore he'd never go back out with me. I don't even know why he broke up with me in the first place. I cried for a week and couldn't even look at him. We got back together three days before his death.

On the day I will never forget, I was going to meet Frank at 4 p.m. at the subway station. I got there an hour early, but as soon as I got there, I felt my heart beating. Sure, my heart always beats, but not like that day. I felt like something was going to happen.

So I went to my house to see if it had to do with my grandmother. She was fine. "I have to go meet Frank," I thought.

When I returned to the station I couldn't hear with all the noise of police sirens and people talking at once. I began to tremble. I tried to speak, but I couldn't. I needed to know what was going on. I knew that it had to do with my friends. I knew my crew always met there, to fight or just chill. I also knew we had enemies. The rival gang. I began to have flashbacks of all the things we did wrong.

My best friend ran over and hugged me. She said in a "please, don't ask" way, "The guys got injured, but they are OK."

"Don't lie to me," I said with tears in my eyes. "He's dead, right?"

None of my friends had the guts to tell me the truth, a truth I felt. They couldn't even look at me. They knew that Frank always said, "I'm gonna die before I reach 18." He used to tell me that he didn't want me to love him so much, 'cause he was gonna die soon. I used to get mad and cry. But I never really paid mind to it. We all talk crazy at some point.

I couldn't walk home by myself. I tried to call home but the number seemed to have been erased from my head. My friend called for me.

My grandmother came to pick me up. At home I stood still, looking at the things Frank had given me, like love letters. I must have read those letters about a dozen times, while holding onto a white teddy bear I had bought him.

That afternoon felt endless. Listening to the songs Frank had dedicated to me and remembering the past were all I seemed to know how to do. Then, the news came on. It was official. Frank was dead. He was stabbed to death. Two other kids had been injured. One was in critical condition; he had received 12 stab wounds but was alive. The other one was just injured in the arm.

I flipped, I screamed, I cried. I needed a "why" and a "how," and a "why him." I couldn't eat, think, speak or sleep. I felt alone, confused, and insane. I had lost someone I loved. I wanted to go with him.

My friends and family were there for me, but I still felt alone. How could God take away the only thing I had? We broke up a few times, but we always ended up back together. Now I knew I had really lost him. Forever.

All I had on my mind was guilt. It was my fault he was dead. If I'd been there, he wouldn't have gotten killed. I would have died for him.

Now I felt destroyed. I shed so many tears, I felt a pain I couldn't possibly get over. I closed myself to everyone. It was a way of punishing myself.

When the phone rang, I hoped it was him. I still couldn't believe he was gone. I didn't want to accept that. He was too young.

At the funeral home I saw him lying so peacefully still. I tried to wake him up. "Frank, wake up, wake up, let's go." He didn't respond. I held onto his cold hands. I brushed his black, thick head of hair. His face was whiter than usual. He felt cold…I had to warm him up. He looked like an angel.

His mother hugged me and told me that it was OK. She was hiding her own pain, because she couldn't see me cry. She told my aunt to please take me away because I was going to get sick.

I did. I started to slam things, I fought everyone who tried to calm me down. They took me to a hospital. I calmed down. Or so they thought. I was really out of it.

The day of his funeral, I was ready to go to school. I hadn't eaten anything and I looked like a zombie. I just didn't want to be home. I wanted to be left alone.

I waited for him in the subway station. He never arrived. I went to school hoping to find him there. I got sick in school, I got sent to the hospital again. (I didn't get to see him go underground. I don't think I was ready, anyway. I couldn't.)

Again I faked like I was OK, but I wasn't. I just didn't want help. I wanted to punish myself. For letting him die. For losing him. For being in a gang. For not having a mother. For letting people abuse me. It all came down on me. All at once.

It wasn't until January that I decided to get help. I was facing too many problems at home. I looked awful. I had tried to kill myself various times. I had stopped eating. I was doing well in school, but cried too much in class. Sometimes I felt lost.

I told my counselor how I felt. He told me that I should try getting hospitalized. He told me that it would help. I was so out of it, I told him just do it. I got hospitalized. I can't say it didn't help, although being lonely made me think more about Frank. While I was in there, I would always think about him.

My therapist, Brian, was really nice. He would tell me to write down what I felt. We also did a lot of drawing. I stayed for a month in the hospital, and I began to get better.

A lot of people were in and out of my life and they each left a seed of hope in me. It took me a few weeks to know that I was going to be OK. All I needed was to believe in myself. I knew I couldn't give up. I knew Frank was and still is watching me from up above. I knew that God was there also. I knew I was going to make it. I still know I will.

When I got out of the hospital, I went straight to a foster home. At first I was sad. After a while I got to experience things I never had before. My foster family made me feel good and my agency was the best. I loved everyone in there. They all helped me sort out my feelings. I was on medication, and it helped me think clearly.

It's been a year since Frank's death. I'm better now. I've pulled myself back together with the help of the hospital, my counselors, and other people who influenced my life.

I still miss Frank and I always will. But now I can deal with it a little better. I know that everything is not going to be perfect from now on, but I'm strong enough to get help.

> **He used to tell me that he didn't want me to love him so much, 'cause he was gonna die soon.**

I thought we would be together forever, but like they say, "Nothing lasts forever." It's a waste that at such a young age his life was taken away.

The other guys who were injured are doing well. They became Christians, and so did half of the rest of the gang. The other half is still doing the wrong things. I guess some people never learn.

The messed up part is not just the fact that Frank's dead, but that it was kids like us who killed him.

One day I might find someone who I will learn to love. Nevertheless, Frank will always live in my heart. Just like he once said, "True love won't die."

Betty was 16 when she wrote this story.

FICTION SPECIAL

The Fallen

"Martin, do you have anything to say for yourself?" Mr. Gates says to me. I can hear anger in his voice.

He's the superintendent of Bluford High School—a large silver-haired man in his late 60s. His lips are pencil thin, and there are bags under his eyes. Bags from listening to stories like mine.

I know he's going to throw me out of Bluford. I can't blame him. All he knows about me is what he's read in the thick folder on his desk.

I can see the pink suspension notices from my seat. He flips through them like he's leafing through an old phone book. I know the words he's reading. I remember the last letter the school district sent to my mother.

> MARTIN LUNA *has on multiple occasions displayed severe behavioral problems in school and on school grounds. He has repeatedly engaged in threatening and hostile confrontations with other students, and he has violated school*

Here's the first chapter from *The Fallen*, by Paul Langan, a novel about teens facing difficult situations like the ones you read about in this book. *The Fallen* is one of many fiction books in the Bluford Series™ by Townsend Press.

attendance policies numerous times. Furthermore, given his most recent outburst, it is the opinion of this district that he poses a threat to students and faculty. As a result, the district recommends that MARTIN LUNA be expelled from Bluford High School.

My mother cried when she got the letter. I found it laying on our kitchen counter stained with tear drops that made the ink bleed. I crumpled it up right then, but it didn't matter. The damage was done.

Today's my hearing—my last chance. "Well?" he says. He's looking at me now. He doesn't even blink.

The auditorium is quiet except for someone coughing as I stand to answer him. I hear my mother sniffle behind me. *I'm so sorry for everything, Ma,* I want to say. I feel guilt clawing at my chest like invisible hands.

"Please don't do this," my mother yells out. "He's a good boy. *Please!*" I turn to see her standing at her seat holding her hands as if she's praying to him. Her nose is running and her voice is trembling. It reminds me of how she was three months ago, the day my little brother died. I close my eyes to push the memories back, but it doesn't work.

"Ms. Luna," Mr. Gates cuts in. "I understand this is difficult for you, but we've already heard what you had to say. Now *please* let your son speak."

My mother sits down, crosses herself, and quietly wipes her eyes. She's never backed down from anything, but this time I know she expects the worst. So do I.

Mr. Gates turns back to me. He closes my folder, drops his pen, and rubs his forehead like he's got a bad headache. I am in trouble. No question about it.

"Mr. Luna, in just two weeks at Bluford High School, you have been in several serious fights. You have cut school, skipped classes, and last Friday in the middle of yet another fight, you struck a teacher. This behavior is unacceptable. Unless there are some *extenuating circumstances*, I'm afraid we have no choice but to expel you. Now, this hearing is your opportunity to tell your side of the story. Martin, what do you have to say for yourself?"

I look up at him because some of his words escape me. Extenuating circumstances? I don't know what they are. But I do know there are reasons why I shoved old Mr. Dooling into a wall, why me and Steve Morris keep fighting, why my anger sometimes explodes like a gunshot.

I never meant for any of it to happen. I know I screwed up, especially when I pushed the teacher. But everything else I did was the best I could do, was the only choice I really had.

There's no way Mr. Gates will ever understand this. His eyes tell me what he thinks—expelling me is the right thing to do. There's no changing his mind. I can see that.

Still, like Vicky said, I gotta try. I take a deep breath and begin telling him the truth, how it started days ago when I stumbled into Bluford a bloody mess . . .

"Oh my God, Martin," Vicky said as she looked at the cut over my eye. Her mouth was wide open and her hands covered her cheeks. "Who did this to you? Was it Steve?"

I shook my head no. I wished she didn't have to see me this way. I could taste blood in my mouth and knew some was on my face. She deserved to know what happened, but I had no time to explain. Frankie and the rest of my crew were on the road, and someone was about to get hurt. I had to do something. Now.

"I'm fine, Vicky. I'll catch up with you later," I said, but my voice cracked into a nasty whisper. I was dizzy. Too many punches to my head.

"Quick, Martin, inside right now," barked Ms. Spencer, our principal. She led me past Vicky straight to the front office. "The rest of you get back to class. There is nothing to see here."

It was almost time for first lunch period, and a small crowd of students had gathered at the front of the school to see my entrance. They looked at me as if I had just shot someone. *What are you starin' at?* I felt like saying, but I had more important things to worry about.

"Ms. Spencer, I need to speak with someone I know. He's a cop. His name is Nelson Ramirez. I need to speak with him. *Now*," I said. She studied my face carefully, not sure whether to trust me.

I couldn't blame her. Where I come from, you don't talk to cops, and you don't expect them to solve problems. I learned that when Huero, my little brother, was killed. For months, my mother and I waited for the police to do something. All we got from them was an apology and some excuses about workload and too many cases.

But Ramirez was different. He was Chicano like us, a friend of my mom's who grew up in the barrio. He held my mom at my brother's funeral and understood that the day Huero died, part of me died too. Where else could I turn?

"I already called the police, Martin." Ms. Spencer said as I collapsed into the squeaky chair in her office. "I called your mother, too. She's on her way," she added.

My headache was getting worse. The last thing I wanted was my mom to see me this way. But I didn't have time to worry about it.

"Call Ramirez," I repeated, rubbing my swollen jaw. "Here's his phone number. Tell him Martin Luna is looking for him." I handed her the crumpled piece of paper he'd given me over the summer.

"Why him?" Ms. Spencer asked, studying the scrap like it was a fake ID card or something. "If you did something wrong, now is the time to tell me so you won't get in any worse trouble."

I wanted to curse her out right there. Behind her wire-rimmed glasses, she couldn't see nothin'. I wasn't afraid of any punishment she could give me. A suspension? A letter? That ain't nothin' compared to watching your brother die in your arms, seeing his blood drip onto your shoes, feeling his skin turn cool in your hands. And now more blood was about to spill.

"There ain't no worse trouble!" I growled, tired of talking to her. I jumped up and reached for her office phone. But my legs were weak, and the room suddenly felt like waves were rolling through the floor. I leaned against the wall to stop from falling.

"*Martin!*" Ms. Spencer yelled, grabbing me and easing me back into the chair. Her eyes were wide with worry.

"*Please*, Ms. Spencer," I said, pointing to the phone.

"Okay, okay. I'm calling him right now. Just sit down and don't move," she said, nervously dialing the numbers. "But if there is something I can do to protect you and the other students in this school, you need to let me know."

Protect me? Too late for that, I wanted to say. The room was spinning. I grabbed the chair to steady myself. "Just call him."

I knew it would come down to this. I knew it the second I agreed to meet my homeboys in the parking lot outside Bluford. Our crew—Frankie, Chago, Junie, and Jesus—were about to do something we had talked about since Huero died. We were going to get revenge.

After months of searching, we found out who shot my brother—a punk named Hector Maldenado. We'd talked about what we'd do all summer. For a while, I dreamed about it night and day. It was the only thing that pushed the hurt away. The only reason I had to get up in the morning.

Don't get me wrong, I ain't a gangbanger. I've stolen a few things and gotten into some fights, but I never did something serious like this before. But everything changed when Huero died. I snapped like an old rubber band.

Frankie Pacheco knew this. He was the oldest and toughest in our crew. He got us guns and showed us what we needed to know. And for a while I was ready to let it all go down like that.

Pop! Pop! Pop!

In Too Deep

Just three shots. A blast of sour gun smoke. The screeching of tires as Frankie's old LeMans pulled away. The same sounds I heard the afternoon Huero died. That would be the end of it.

But I couldn't do it.

In my head, I kept seeing my brother's face, Vicky's eyes, my Mom's tears. And I kept hearing something my English teacher, Mr. Mitchell, said. You could have a bright future ahead of you. *Don't throw it away.*

Call me soft. I don't care. You're not the one who sits at your brother's grave, listens to your mother crying in the dark, and knows what it's like to lose someone. If you were, you'd understand why I couldn't be like the coward who drove down our street and stole my brother's life with a gunshot.

"Yes, this message is for Officer Ramirez," Ms. Spencer said. "This is the principal at Bluford High School. I have Martin Luna here in my office. He seems to have been involved in an altercation and wishes to speak with you. He says it's important."

I put my head in my hands. A message! Where was he? It was the one time I needed to reach him, and he wasn't there.

Call me anytime, he had said when he gave me the number. Yeah, right.

I felt Ms. Spencer watching me. I knew she was wishing I never transferred into her school. But if I'd stayed at Zamora High, I'd be in jail or dead already.

That's why my mom moved out of our old neighborhood, making me start my sophomore year at Bluford High. I was so angry when she told me, I almost punched her. Can you believe that? I hate when I get that way, but Huero's death did that to me.

The move added 45 minutes to her bus ride to Wal-Mart where she worked as a cashier with Nilsa, Frankie's older sister. But she did it—to *save* me. It didn't work.

"Where is he?" a man yelled into the office, shattering my thoughts. "Where's Martin?"

I looked up to see Mr. Mitchell. The throbbing in my skull

was worsening by the minute, and the room was fuzzy, like an old TV that isn't tuned in right.

"What happened?" he asked, shaking his head. The other day, he gave me an "A" for an essay I wrote about Huero. I wondered what he'd say if he knew another kid was about to die because I was too scared to talk.

I stared at him, my heart pounding. My hands sweating. The room seemed to spin. Overhead, the bell sounded announcing the beginning of first lunch period. Time was running out like blood from a cut.

"Martin, what is it?"

I knew it would take Frankie at least a half hour to get to Hector's house. It hadn't been that long since we fought. If I acted now, there still was a chance I could do something. But I wasn't ready to rat out my boys. I ain't a snitch.

Up until a month ago, Frankie and I were like brothers. *Family*, he called me and the rest of our crew. I even took a beating to earn that word. That's how we did things.

But then Frankie admitted that the bullet that killed my brother was probably aimed at him. I don't know why I never thought of it before, but it made sense. Frankie was the one with the knife wound, the homie most feared on our block, the tattoo-covered 19-yearold who had enemies everywhere. Of course the bullet was meant for him, not an eight-year-old boy. Not Huero.

The news changed me. It was like I'd been asleep and suddenly woke up. Questions kept popping in my head in the middle of the night, cutting our friendship like a knife. Making me secretly hate him. Why did Huero have to pay for what Frankie did? And why was Frankie free to cruise the 'hood while my brother's lying in the ground?

Frankie wasn't stupid. He knew I was changing. That's why he wanted me to do the shooting this morning. It would make me as guilty as him, and it would mean he'd always have something on me in case I gave him trouble. I'm sure he planned it this way.

In Too Deep

But he didn't plan on me backing out.

"I'm not doin' it, Frankie. I'm serious," I announced while we were all sitting in his LeMans ready to get Hector. The car got as quiet as a grave.

You should have seen Frankie's face. If it were a gun, I'd be dead right now. I jumped out before anyone could stop me.

Chago, my best friend from back in the day, tried to change my mind. He was worried about what Frankie would do next.

"C'mon, Martin. We're family, man. Brothers," Chago said. "Let's go."

The word stung me. *Family*. It was like a slap in my face. Look what the word did to me—it cost me my brother and was about to turn me into a criminal. That ain't what family is supposed to be. Anyone who says so needs to get their head examined.

"My brother was Huero, Chago," I said. "And he's dead because of something Frankie did. You know it's true. What we are about to do, it ain't family, Chago. It's crazy."

Frankie lost it. His jaw tightened up, and he got this cold look I saw once before when he jumped a kid for talking to his girlfriend. The guy was already on the ground when Frankie's foot smashed into his face with a heavy wet thud. I can still hear the sound. The guy moaned and threw up, and Frankie backed away, acting like he was trying to protect his new steel tipped boots from the mess. Like they were more important than another person.

Frankie was ready to do worse to me when he stepped out of his car. Don't get me wrong. I can handle myself in a fight. But I'm no match for Frankie. His fists pounded into my face and side, knocking me to my knees. That's when he pulled out his gun.

"You can't leave your family, Martin," he said. His nine millimeter was pointed at my face. It was the first time I looked into the barrel of a gun.

All I could think about was the bloody mess I'd be when my mother found me, how she'd cry at my funeral with no sons at her side.

"I can't go no further. Do what you gotta do," I said. I whispered a prayer just in case.

Frankie blinked.

Maybe it was the guilt he had for Huero's death. Maybe it was that he didn't want to shoot me in daylight where a crowd of people could witness it. Or maybe it was because he was shocked that I was willing to die to prove I ain't a killer. I don't know what it was, but Frankie let me go.

"This ain't done," he growled and jumped back into his car.

I believe him.

The clock over Ms. Spencer's desk said 10:38. Frankie and the boys had been on the road for 20 minutes already. There were at least two guns in the car, and the only one who knew their plan was me. I was wasting time.

"C'mon, Martin. It's like I said before. You have a choice. You can end this right now," Mr. Mitchell said, staring at me like I was a puzzle. "We're listening."

I could feel myself zoning out, like there was a fog settling over my brain. All last night, I replayed how this day would go down. When I grabbed my bandana and left to meet Frankie, I knew I had to walk away, that Frankie was gonna come at me like never before. But I figured if I could just escape and get to Bluford, it would all be over.

I was wrong.

Looking at Ms. Spencer's tight jaw and Mr. Mitchell's wide eyes, I knew it was just beginning.

The Fallen, a Bluford Series™ novel, is reprinted with permission from Townsend Press. Copyright © 2002.

Want to read more? This and other *Bluford Series*™ novels and paperbacks can be purchased for $1 each at www.townsendpress.com.

Teens:
How to Get More Out of This Book

Self-help: The teens who wrote the stories in this book did so because they hope that telling their stories will help readers who are facing similar challenges. They want you to know that you are not alone, and that taking specific steps can help you manage or overcome very difficult situations. They've done their best to be clear about the actions that worked for them so you can see if they'll work for you.

Writing: You can also use the book to improve your writing skills. Each teen in this book wrote 5-10 drafts of his or her story before it was published. If you read the stories closely you'll see that the teens work to include a beginning, a middle, and an end, and good scenes, description, dialogue, and anecdotes (little stories). To improve your writing, take a look at how these writers construct their stories. Try some of their techniques in your own writing.

Reading: Finally, you'll notice that we include the first chapter from a Bluford Series novel in this book, alongside the true stories by teens. We hope you'll like it enough to continue reading. The more you read, the more you'll strengthen your reading skills. Teens at Youth Communication like the Bluford novels because they explore themes similar to those in their own stories. Your school may already have the Bluford books. If not, you can order them online for only $1.

Resources on the Web

We will occasionally post Think About It questions on our website, www.youthcomm.org, to accompany stories in this and other Youth Communication books. We try out the questions with teens and post the ones they like best. Many teens report that writing answers to those questions in a journal is very helpful.

How to Use This Book in Staff Training

Staff say that reading these stories gives them greater insight into what teens are thinking and feeling, and new strategies for working with them. You can help the staff you work with by using these stories as case studies.

Select one story to read in the group, and ask staff to identify and discuss the main issue facing the teen. There may be disagreement about this, based on the background and experience of staff. That is fine. One point of the exercise is that teens have complex lives and needs. Adults can probably be more effective if they don't focus too narrowly and can see several dimensions of their clients.

Ask staff: What issues or feelings does the story provoke in them? What kind of help do they think the teen wants? What interventions are likely to be most promising? Least effective? Why? How would you build trust with the teen writer? How have other adults failed the teen, and how might that affect his or her willingness to accept help? What other resources would be helpful to this teen, such as peer support, a mentor, counseling, family therapy, etc.

Resources on the Web

From time to time we will post Think About It questions on our website, www.youthcomm.org, to accompany stories in this and other Youth Communication books. We try out the questions with teens and post the ones that they find most effective. We'll also post lesson for some of the stories. Adults can use the questions and lessons in workshops.

Discussion Guide

Teachers and Staff:
How to Use This Book in Groups

When working with teens individually or in groups, using these stories can help young people face difficult issues in a way that feels safe to them. That's because talking about the issues in the stories usually feels safer to teens than talking about those same issues in their own lives. Addressing issues through the stories allows for some personal distance; they hit close to home, but not too close. Talking about them opens up a safe place for reflection. As teens gain confidence talking about the issues in the stories, they usually become more comfortable talking about those issues in their own lives.

Below are general questions that can help you lead discussions about the stories, which help teens and staff reflect on the issues in their own work and lives. In most cases you can read a story and conduct a discussion in one 45-minute session. Teens are usually happy to read the stories aloud, with each teen reading a paragraph or two. (Allow teens to pass if they don't want to read.) It takes 10-15 minutes to read a story straight through. However, it is often more effective to let workshop participants make comments and discuss the story as you go along. The workshop leader may even want to annotate her copy of the story beforehand with key questions.

If teens read the story ahead of time or silently, it's good to break the ice with a few questions that get everyone on the same page: Who is the main character? How old is she? What happened to her? How did she respond? Etc. Another good starting question is: "What stood out for you in the story?" Go around the room and let each person briefly mention one thing.

Then move on to open-ended questions, which encourage participants to think more deeply about what the writers were feeling, the choices they faced, and they actions they took. There are no right or wrong answers to the open-ended questions. Open-ended questions encourage participants to think about how the themes, emotions and choices in the stories relate to their own lives. Here are some examples of open-ended questions that we have found to be effective. You can use variations of these questions with almost any story in this book.

—What main problem or challenge did the writer face?

—What choices did the teen have in trying to deal with the problem?

—Which way of dealing with the problem was most effective for the teen? Why?

—What strengths, skills, or resources did the teen use to address the challenge?

—If you were in the writer's shoes, what would you have done?

—What could adults have done better to help this young person?

—What have you learned by reading this story that you didn't know before?

—What, if anything, will you do differently after reading this story?

—What surprised you in this story?

—Do you have a different view of this issue, or see a different way of dealing with it, after reading this story? Why or why not?

Credits

The stories in this book originally appeared in the following Youth Communication publications:

"Rebels Without a Cause: Two Days with a Posse," By Anonymous, *New Youth Connections*, Sept./Oct. 1988

"Whatever Become of the Untouchables?" By Anonymous, *New Youth Connections*, November 1990

"My Boyfriend Was a (Latin) King," by Anonymous, *New Youth Connections*, April 2000

"Down With the Decepts," by Christopher Bogle, *Foster Care Youth United*, Sept./Oct. 1996

"My 'Gang-Related' Weekend," by Anonymous, *Foster Care Youth United*, November/December 1998

"The Real Deal on Gangs," by Anonymous, *Foster Care Youth United*, November/December 1998

"Crewsin' for a Bruisin,'" by Troy Shawn Welcome, *New Youth Connections*, April 1994

"The Life and Times of a Decepticon," by David Quiles Guzman, *New Youth Connections*, March 1990

"Remembering Mike," by Carlos Lavezzari, *New Youth Connections*, May 1992

"In Too Deep," by Philip Hodge, *New Youth Connections*, March 2000

"Almost One of the Gang," by Anonymous, *New Youth Connections*, December 2007

"My Crew Was My Family," by Xavier Reyes, *New Youth Connections*, March/April 1994

"When Things Get Hectic," by Juan Azize, *New Youth Connections*, April 1994

"True Love Won't Die," by Betty Dominguez, *Foster Care Youth United*, July/August 1999

About Youth Communication

Youth Communication, founded in 1980, is a nonprofit youth development program located in New York City whose mission is to teach writing, journalism, and leadership skills. The teenagers we train become writers for our websites and books and for two print magazines, *New Youth Connections*, a general-interest youth magazine, and *Represent*, a magazine by and for young people in foster care.

Each year, up to 100 young people participate in Youth Communication's school-year and summer journalism workshops where they work under the direction of full-time professional editors. Most are African American, Latino, or Asian, and many are recent immigrants. The opportunity to reach their peers with accurate portrayals of their lives and important self-help information motivates the young writers to create powerful stories.

Our goal is to run a strong youth development program in which teens produce high quality stories that inform and inspire their peers. Doing so requires us to be sensitive to the complicated lives and emotions of the teen participants while also providing an intellectually rigorous experience. We achieve that goal in the writing/teaching/editing relationship, which is the core of our program.

Our teaching and editorial process begins with discussions

between adult editors and the teen staff. In those meetings, the teens and the editors work together to identify the most important issues in the teens' lives and to figure out how those issues can be turned into stories that will resonate with teen readers.

Once story topics are chosen, students begin the process of crafting their stories. For a personal story, that means revisiting events in one's past to understand their significance for the future. For a commentary, it means developing a logical and persuasive point of view. For a reported story, it means gathering information through research and interviews. Students look inward and outward as they try to make sense of their experiences and the world around them and find the points of intersection between personal and social concerns. That process can take a few weeks or a few months. Stories frequently go through ten or more drafts as students work under the guidance of their editors, the way any professional writer does.

Many of the students who walk through our doors have uneven skills, as a result of poor education, living under extremely stressful conditions, or coming from homes where English is a second language. Yet, to complete their stories, students must successfully perform a wide range of activities, including writing and rewriting, reading, discussion, reflection, research, interviewing, and typing. They must work as members of a team and they must accept individual responsibility. They learn to provide constructive criticism, and to accept it. They engage in explorations of truthfulness, fairness, and accuracy. They meet deadlines. They must develop the audacity to believe that they have something important to say and the humility to recognize that saying it well is not a process of instant gratification. Rather, it usually requires a long, hard struggle through many discussions and much rewriting.

It would be impossible to teach these skills and dispositions as separate, disconnected topics, like grammar, ethics, or assertiveness. However, we find that students make rapid progress when they are learning skills in the context of an inquiry that is personally significant to them and that will benefit their peers.

When teens publish their stories—in *New Youth Connections* and *Represent,* on the web, and in other publications—they reach tens of thousands of teen and adult readers. Teachers, counselors, social workers, and other adults circulate the stories to young people in their classes and out-of-school youth programs. Adults tell us that teens in their programs—including many who are ordinarily resistant to reading—clamor for the stories. Teen readers report that the stories give them information they can't get anywhere else, and inspire them to reflect on their lives and open lines of communication with adults.

Writers usually participate in our program for one semester, though some stay much longer. Years later, many of them report that working here was a turning point in their lives—that it helped them acquire the confidence and skills that they needed for success in college and careers. Scores of our graduates have overcome tremendous obstacles to become journalists, writers, and novelists. They include National Book Award finalist Edwidge Danticat, novelist Ernesto Quinonez, writer Veronica Chambers and *New York Times* reporter Rachel Swarns. Hundreds more are working in law, business, and other careers. Many are teachers, principals, and youth workers, and several have started nonprofit youth programs themselves and work as mentors—helping another generation of young people develop their skills and find their voices.

Youth Communication is a nonprofit educational corporation. Contributions are gratefully accepted and are tax deductible to the fullest extent of the law.

To make a contribution, or for information about our publications and programs, including our catalog of over 100 books and curricula for hard-to-reach teens, see www.youthcomm.org

About The Editors

Al Desetta has been an editor of Youth Communication's two teen magazines, *Foster Care Youth United* (now known as *Represent*) and *New Youth Connections*. He was also an instructor in Youth Communication's juvenile prison writing program. In 1991, he became the organization's first director of teacher development, working with high school teachers to help them produce better writers and student publications.

Prior to working at Youth Communication, Desetta directed environmental education projects in New York City public high schools and worked as a reporter.

He has a master's degree in English literature from City College of the City University of New York and a bachelor's degree from the State University of New York at Binghamton, and he was a Revson Fellow at Columbia University for the 1990-91 academic year.

He is the editor of many books, including several other Youth Communication anthologies: *The Heart Knows Something Different: Teenage Voices from the Foster Care System, The Struggle to Be Strong,* and *The Courage to Be Yourself.* He is currently a freelance editor.

Keith Hefner co-founded Youth Communication in 1980 and has directed it ever since. He is the recipient of the Luther P. Jackson Education Award from the New York Association of Black Journalists and a MacArthur Fellowship. He was also a Revson Fellow at Columbia University.

Laura Longhine is the editorial director at Youth Communication. She edited *Represent*, Youth Communication's magazine by and for youth in foster care, for three years, and has written for a variety of publications. She has a BA in English from Tufts University and an MS in Journalism from Columbia University.

More Helpful Books From Youth Comunication

The Struggle to Be Strong: True Stories by Teens About Overcoming Tough Times. Foreword by Veronica Chambers. Help young people identify and build on their own strengths with 30 personal stories about resiliency. (Free Spirit)

Starting With "I": Personal Stories by Teenagers. "Who am I and who do I want to become?" Thirty-five stories examine this question through the lens of race, ethnicity, gender, sexuality, family, and more. Increase this book's value with the free Teacher's Guide, available from youthcomm.org. (Youth Communication)

Real Stories, Real Teens. Inspire teens to read and recognize their strengths with this collection of 26 true stories by teens. The young writers describe how they overcame significant challenges and stayed true to themselves. Also includes the first chapters from three novels in the Bluford Series. (Youth Communication)

The Courage to Be Yourself: True Stories by Teens About Cliques, Conflicts, and Overcoming Peer Pressure. In 26 first-person stories, teens write about their lives with searing honesty. These stories will inspire young readers to reflect on their own lives, work through their problems, and help them discover who they really are. (Free Spirit)

Out With It: Gay and Straight Teens Write About Homosexuality. Break stereotypes and provide support with this unflinching look at gay life from a teen's perspective. With a focus on urban youth, this book also includes several heterosexual teens' transformative experiences with gay peers. (Youth Communication)

 *Things Get Hectic: Teens Write About the Violence That Surrounds Them.* Violence is commonplace in many teens' lives, be it bullying, gangs, dating, or family relationships. Hear the experiences of victims, perpetrators, and witnesses through more than 50 real-world stories. (Youth Communication)

From Dropout to Achiever: Teens Write About School. Help teens overcome the challenges of graduating, which may involve overcoming family problems, bouncing back from a bad semester, or even dropping out for a time. These teens show how they achieve academic success. (Youth Communication)

 *My Secret Addiction: Teens Write About Cutting.* These true accounts of cutting, or self-mutilation, offer a window into the personal and family situations that lead to this secret habit, and show how teens can get the help they need. (Youth Communication)

Sticks and Stones: Teens Write About Bullying. Shed light on bullying, as told from the perspectives of the perpetrator, the victim, and the witness. These stories show why bullying occurs, the harm it causes, and how it might be prevented. (Youth Communication)

 *Boys to Men: Teens Write About Becoming a Man.* The young men in this book write about confronting the challenges of growing up. Their honesty and courage make them role models for teens who are bombarded with contradictory messages about what it means to be a man. (Youth Communication)

Through Thick and Thin: Teens Write About Obesity, Eating Disorders, and Self Image. Help teens who struggle with obesity, eating disorders, and body weight issues. These stories show the pressures teens face when they are confronted by unrealistic standards for physical appearance, and how emotions can affect the way we eat. (Youth Communication)

To order these and other books, go to:
www.youthcomm.org
or call 212-279-0708 x115

www.ingramcontent.com/pod-product-compliance
Lightning Source LLC
Chambersburg PA
CBHW071729090426
42738CB00011B/2422